D1366581

WOMEN *of* VISION

WOMEN *of* VISION

Beatrice Johns

ImagineInk Publishing Company, Inc.

ImagineInk Publishing Company, Inc.
2178 East Pitman Avenue
Wentzville MO 63385-3712

Copyright © 2004 by Beatrice Johns
Edited by Deborah Bowman
Cover Design by Larry Marshall
Cover photograph courtesy of Children's Mercy Hospital

All rights reserved, no part of this book may be reproduced in any form without written permission from the publisher, except for brief passages included in a review appearing in a newspaper or magazine with permission from the publisher.

Library of Congress Control Number: 2003116171
ISBN: 0-9724257-2-1

Permission to reprint photographs and documents was granted by Children's Mercy Hospital.

For additional copies of

Women of Vision

$15.95 U.S., $19.95 Canada, plus $2.50 S&H to:
ImagineInk Publishing Company, Inc.
2178 East Pitman Avenue
Wentzville, MO 63385-3712

Dealers - Bookstores - Quantity Buyers
Call, write, fax, or e-mail for volume discount information
Phone: 636-639-8989
Fax: 636-639-8990
E-mail: info@imagineinkpublishing.com

Acknowledgements

A special thanks to Children's Mercy Hospital; Jennifer Benz, Media Relations Coordinator; and Barbara Mueth, Vice President of Community Relations. Also thanks to Dr. Ned Smull and to Eric Jones, prior Hospital Director.

Thanks for an open door for one day, Steve Byers, Mercy Resource Development, and Carol Belt, Mercy Nurse.

Thanks to Ann Peppard White for the interview regarding her personal experiences with Dr. Richardson.

Thanks to *The Kansas City Star* for their articles from various editions, and to The Kansas City Public Library.

Women *of* Vision

Author's Experience (Preface)

Women Professionals of 1897   1

Getting Started   6

Kate First   9

Dr. Katherine Berry Richardson's Age Was?   12

Troost Hospital   14

414 North Highland Avenue   15

121 Clinton Place   20

Mercy's Messenger   21

Ann's Pageant   24

Mr. Loose Visits Dr. Richardson   29

The Independence and Woodland Hospital   31

Mercy's Children   37

The Ill Children of Mercy Hospital   45

Wheatley-Provident Hospital   50

Mercy's Clubs   54

Experiences of Katherine Berry Richardson   60

Begging for Mercy Hospital   66

Passing   71

Doctors for Mercy   73

Dr. Richardson and *The Kansas City Star* Newspaper   76

Troy's Story   79

The Polio Epidemic   81

Problem Solving   84

Nursing History 88

Mercy's Nurses 91

Nurses' Hall 96

The Alpine Lamp 99

Growing Older 101

Dr. Katherine Berry Richardson's Death 103

Mercy Lives 105

Try a Greener Day:
My Series of Stays

Arriving at Mercy 110

My First Days 113

Inspections 118

Daily Life at Mercy 120

Sick Again 123

Going to School 126

Life at Mercy Continues 130

Back Home and Back Again 134

Grace 137

Sicker Than Ever 141

Christmas at Mercy 145

Friends 151

Home for Good 154

Author's Experience

The Children's Mercy Hospital in Kansas City, Missouri played a basic role in my life. In 1928 it was a charity hospital. When I became ill, our family doctor tried many treatments and medications, but to no avail.

Our mother, father, and we four children were living in a small three-room house. We were poor, so when my parents heard of Mercy Hospital, they decided to try it as a last resort.

Driving the fifty miles to Kansas City was a major undertaking in 1928. My mother did not drive and had never been to the city, so my Uncle Harry drove us to the hospital, where I stayed for three months. That became a pattern that went on for five years. I did not get well, but I stayed alive.

During my time in the hospital, I met Dr. Richardson, one of its founders. To me she seemed a kind, older doctor who both talked to us and listened to us. She was not my doctor.

My disease was called many types of anemia. The diagnosis given me fifty-one years later was Crohn's disease, and I now have medication that helps me to live a much less painful life.

Doing research on Children's Mercy Hospital has been an interesting undertaking. The hospital, founded and run by women in 1897, has become a huge Children's Hospital run by men. It is no longer a charity hospital, but its staff still cures thousands of children every year, and of course some are charity patients.

—Bea Johns

Women Professionals of 1897

Alice Berry Graham, dentist, and Katherine Berry Graham Richardson, M.D., moved from LaCrosse, Wisconsin to Kansas City, Missouri in 1895. They rented rooms for office space and living quarters in the Ridge Building. Dr. Richardson's husband, an invalid, came with them. He died in 1898.

The Berry sisters were extraordinary women in many ways. The barriers they overcame is a story in itself. Women of their day were fighting for a vote, prohibition, and laws granting married women control of their property and money. They were fighting to be accepted as adult human beings. It was an uphill battle.

Religion helped women in some ways, but most Christian leaders also considered women and children subject to their men: husbands, fathers, and so forth. The newspapers made fun of women who went into business. This "sense of humor" was intended to discourage any woman who worked outside the home. There was a complete set of rules a woman had to follow if she wanted to be considered a lady. Correct posture, whether sitting or standing, was a must for a lady. Many women had walked with a book on their heads as girls.

Alice and Kate were ladies and were considered as such by the people they dealt with, even though the public frowned on their professions for women. Both sisters worked with men and women; they had both sexes on their hospital board. The fact that they were widows helped them succeed. The law allowed widows to control their own money by 1897. They were both willing to battle the odds, and neither woman had any intention of being submissive to anyone.

When they started working with the ill, poor children, not much was known about pediatric medicine. Children were treated as small adults; they were simply given smaller amounts of the adult medication, hoping for the cure. Alice and Kate were striding into an open field of medicine.

The physician and dental societies of Kansas City in 1897 excluded women. The women found no welcome from the American Medical Association (AMA) or the dental society. Only men

Katherine Berry Richardson

Courtesy Children's Mercy Hospital

had that privilege. No woman doctor or dentist was allowed to cross the threshold of a hospital or dental office as a part of the professional community.

Kate and Alice took rooms for their living quarters and hung out their shingle. They had high hopes of patients coming in their doors. None came. No doctor or dentist in Kansas City of 1897 would think of referring a patient to a woman professional, no matter how well they would be treated.

The women were about to give up when one evening Alice went out on an errand and heard a child crying. She began to investigate and found a newborn baby in the trash barrel. It was a dirty, smelly infant; she picked it up and took it home. The two women cleaned up the little girl and took care of her until they put her in a hospital. That was the first child the sisters cared for.

That first child was ill and abandoned, and the sisters began to see the need for good care of ill children. The sisters knew these children needed their help, but how to help them? Dr. Kate began going to patients' homes.

The patriarchal walls built around women were very high. In 1897 the patriarchal society was set on maintaining the status quo. Women stayed in the home and cared for their children and husbands. The married woman could not own property, nor could she keep her children if her husband divorced her. She could not divorce him. She could not take out a lease on a building, write a check, or get a bank loan in her own name. There were male explanations for this state of affairs. Women were small and weak; they needed the superior male to think and act for them. Women were thought to have smaller brains; therefore, they could not think great thoughts, as men could. Altogether, women were inferior, needing care and guidance from the males in their families.

Alice Berry Graham

Courtesy Children's Mercy Hospital

In the 1800's, men had secret societies in which they could network with each other, excluding women and unacceptable men. A woman going into business in 1897, as Kate and Alice were trying to do, had no network to turn to, in either male or female society. The total lack of male-female communication worked against them. Men monopolized positions of authority in those days. Women had to petition a judge before opening a hospital, buying a house, or beginning a business. Quite often the judge treated the women with disdain, turning down their petitions as unnecessary.

The sisters had recognized a large gap in the 1897 society. Bright but ill and crippled children were ignored by society. Kate and Alice knew they would need help after the second child Alice found abandoned on the street needed hospitalization. She paid five dollars a day for that child and some others, but she knew their very short funds could not take care of all the children who needed hospitalization.

They decided to ask for help. They began to speak to various women's groups, asking for money to care for these children, explaining the need for help with poverty patients and bright children who, with operations, could become productive, happy adults. They had an uphill battle. The early churches preached that the people who died of venereal disease, died as a judgment for their evil deeds, and children who died of these same diseases, died because of the sins of the fathers. Many people believed this philosophy in those days because they didn't believe or didn't even know about the germ theory. Men and women believed their ministers.

Doctors Kate and Alice could not vote. The politicians of that time spoke eloquently of the weakness of woman's character as affecting their judgment. The very idea of a woman voting was laughable. The Suffragists did not agree with that theory. They were fighting for education, political representation, and equal rights in legal affairs and property laws. Alice and Kate agreed with the Suffragists.

Kate and Alice found their vocation for saving helpless, ill children from that first child Alice brought home from the trash barrel. They did not deviate from their self-decided goal to make crippled, poor children well. They only asked whether the children were poor and whether they were ill.

One of their many challenges was the AMA. The American Medical Association adopted a code of ethics in medicine in 1847. These learned gentlemen stated that doctors should unite tenderness with firmness and condescension with authority. They concluded this attitude would inspire the minds of their patients with gratitude, respect, and confidence. This patrician ideal became a commercial tool.

These doctors of 1847 intended to exclude women, blacks, and poor men from medical training. They did condescend, after some discussion, to let a few black men into doctors' training, because white doctors did not want to treat black people. Midwives were outlawed and prices were raised for medical training beyond reason to discourage poor students. The AMA set up a series of committees to close what they considered to be irregular schools. Those were the schools that accepted blacks, women, and middle-class men. Medicine by these new rules became a business of the white male elite.

At one point, the AMA decided that doctors needed to police themselves. However, in 1899, a Dr. J .D. Stubbs, M.D., wrote, "I warn you not to uncover the mistakes of a fellow practitioner." From that day forward doctors turned their eyes away from wrongdoing by members of the AMA.

The world Alice and Kate stepped into in 1897 was a battleground, but they stepped forward with courage. Two petite and determined women started a new kind of hospital in Kansas City, Missouri.

Getting Started

The road had deep ruts, making it difficult for walkers to cross the street. The old house was in a bad neighborhood. There were several out-buildings and an old, partly fallen-down barn in the back yard. To add to the property's dilapidated appearance, there were long, wooden stairs going up from the street. This maternity and children's hospital had been opened in 1875 by the Women's Christian Temperance Union. The women of the union gave money to keep the hospital open. This women and children's hospital closed in 1896 and was rechartered in 1897 with the same management and board of directors. Its charity work was limited to a free ward for children. Dr. Graham took the first ill child to this hospital. It was a very small but important beginning.

After an operation, the first little girl was able to go to an orphanage. The success with their first child of the streets caused the sisters to decide to take another ill and abandoned child to the same hospital where they could rent a bed.

Coutresy Children's Mercy Hospital

The hospital was in financial trouble and decided to close its doors. Dr. Anna Canfield Smith called a meeting with the sisters, and she offered to turn over thirteen dollars of usable equipment with the hospital sale. They accepted the offer because the hospital had an unexpired license. The Women's Hospital had an operating license, and this meant they did not have to get permission from the board for a new license. The fact that this hospital was used for women treated by only women doctors added to its value for the sisters. Every bed was filled with maternity patients when they bought the hospital. The sisters changed the hospital slowly to a children's hospital and kept the managing power in their own names. The hospital came with a nursing school, and it continued training nurses. The first hospital was named, "Free Bed Fund Association for Crippled, Deformed, and Ruptured Children." The word free appealed to many poor parents with ill children.

The sisters had joined a popular group called, "The Bands of Mercy." These groups were formed to protect children and to promote kindness to animals. The Kansas City group's leader was Edwin R. Weeks. During a Band of Mercy meeting on April 28, 1899, at the Convention Center, Alice Graham asked whether she could use the name of the association for her new hospital. Mr. Weeks told her it would be a compliment to his group. The sisters named their hospital The Children's Mercy Hospital.

A cartoon appeared in *The Kansas City Star* shortly after the sisters opened their hospital. It showed Dr. Richardson on a ladder with her skirts pinned up, a cloth tied around her head, and her mouth open, directing operations below her while waving a dust rag. The caption of this two-column cartoon read, "Only women—a hospital where men are to be entirely excluded."

The people of Kansas City took note of the hospital, so different from the male-operated hospitals of Kansas City. They began to drive by to see a strange group of women who dared own and keep a working hospital. Out-of-town sightseers were brought by in groups. It was a wonder for Kansas City.

The hospital had wood floors, coal stoves, and no indoor plumbing. The sisters and nurses did the cleaning, brought in the coal, took out the ashes, and did general housework, in addition to taking care of the little patients that came in from the first day.

After buying a hospital, the sisters needed a staff. They hired all women. These women worked hard, sometimes without pay.

The hospital still did not receive acceptance in Kansas City. These "uppity women" were reprimanded by Kansas City for not staying home, which was considered to be a woman's place. The papers and businessmen made sharp remarks. Their daily path was strewn with thorns. The dilapidated hospital stayed open, and free care for poor, ill, and bright children went on. The only part of the hospital that received acceptance by the public was free care for poor and ill children.

The sisters knew they could not keep the hospital open without help. Their own small funds were not enough to keep even this small hospital going. They spoke to their board and decided to approach the churches and societies of Kansas City, asking for help for their poor and deserving children, who, when well, would become productive citizens. From then on, Doctors Graham and Richardson went out to speak in churches and schools asking for aid for their hospital. Dr. Richardson thought Kansas City should help its children.

In this first hospital, because these women did all of the cleaning, laundry, and cooking, they could feed a child for ninety cents a day. Every morning Dr. Alice took two large baskets to the Farmers Market. She boarded a streetcar and filled the baskets with fruit and vegetables, boarded the return streetcar and, with help from the motorman, got off at the hospital. She was ready to feed the children, nurses, and other workers for the day.

Laundry was done by hand with no indoor water source, so carrying and heating water for even a small hospital must have been daunting. The homemade lye cake soap had to be cut up and boiled into liquid form. From their first day in the hospital the sisters kept books; every penny taken in or spent was accounted for. They were good businesswomen.

Kate First

During their high school years, Alice and Kate talked of getting a college education. They knew their father could not help them, even though he encouraged their efforts. Kate wanted to be a doctor and Alice wanted to be a dentist. Both professions were almost unheard of for women in the 1800's. Alice said she would teach while Kate went to college if, upon her completion, Kate would put her through dental college. Kate agreed.

In the 1800's and into the early 1900's, young men and women could graduate from high school, and by taking a county teacher's test at the nearest courthouse they could become teachers. When they passed, they received a temporary teaching certificate. A large number of poor young people became teachers in this way. By going to school in the summer, they could gain their degrees in nine years or so. Alice probably started teaching after high school. Kate chose Mount Union College in Alliance, Ohio. She tutored other students to help pay her way through college. Alice continued teaching to pay Kate's basic tuition.

Kate graduated with a Bachelor of Philosophy and a Master's degree in Psychology. Sister Alice taught on while Kate chose Pennsylvania Women's College in Philadelphia for work on her doctor's degree. Again Kate tutored other students while working on her own degree. There were times she had to put newspaper in her shoes because they were worn out and she could not afford new ones. Nothing discouraged either woman; hardship seemed to encourage them.

During her years of teaching and sharing earnings with Kate, Alice gave money for the care of ill and crippled poor children. Both women endured poverty in order to attain their future.

Kate had only one black dress for school and dress up. She had wanted a nice white dress for graduation, but had no money for another dress. Going to medical school meant going without all of the things a young woman would like to have. Kate kept right on going to school until she attained her medical degree.

Graduation day came; sadly, Kate cleaned her old black dress carefully then ran an errand just before the ceremony. When she came back to her room she found a lovely white dress on her bed. She put it on, thankfully. She never found out who gave it to her.

Kate's thesis is almost unreadable, in the copy sent by her school. The first page states the subject, "Puerperal Troubles. Submitted to the faculty of the Women's College of Pennsylvania, for the degree of Doctor of Medicine, by Katherine D. Berry-Class of 1887."

Kate wrote in a large, careful hand. She tried to tell the young mothers she was treating how beautiful they were. She concluded that no amount of compliments from doctors or friends convinced them. She disapproved the practice of a nine-month bed rest for pregnancy. She stated the need of exercise for both mother and child, to improve circulation and to avoid puerperal eclampsia. Neither she nor her teachers had an explanation for what she called, "This dreaded condition." She disagreed with country doctors who did not examine urine samples.

During those early eighties, Adolph Semmelweiss was working on this same women's fever and came to the conclusion that handwashing before treating or operating on patients would save their lives. The doctors of that day just laughed at such a simple solution. Women continued to die from lack of the doctors' handwashing, but Dr. Richardson believed Adolph Semmelweiss was right. She became an advocate for cleanliness.

Kate had her M.D. degree and immediately started teaching to put Alice through school. Alice had been married and lost her husband during those teaching years. Alice did not go to school right away because the sisters were out of money. She entered dental college in 1889. Her school had only male students when she entered Philadelphia Dental College and Hospital of Oral Surgery, on Cherry above Seventh Street, in Philadelphia, Pennsylvania.

Alice was the only woman in a class of fifty-seven students. Classes were surely a challenge for her, but she was a determined woman. She succeeded where other women feared to tread or when they were not allowed in the school. She graduated in 1890. Alice wrote her thesis on the extraction of teeth. She did tutoring while attending college and continued to give part of her earnings to poor children.

The great day had arrived; both sisters were educated in their chosen professions, but where to start practice? They studied maps and could not decide where to go. They wrote down the names of towns they could afford to travel to and laid the papers on the floor. They threw coins at the names of towns, and one coin landed on LaCrosse, Wisconsin. They went there to start their practice.

Dr. Katherine Berry Richardson's Age Was?

Dr. Kate's age has been a bone of contention for years. There is a story of the Flatrock Court House being burned, but that is not verified. Many courthouses were burned during the Civil War, so it could be true.

Some research shows Stephen P. Berry and Harriet Benson Berry as parents of Alice Berry in Warren, Pennsylvania in 1850. A second child, Claire, was born in 1856.

The family moved to Flatrock, Kentucky in Bourbon County. There were three towns named Flatrock in Kentucky. The Berry family's Flatrock appeared in the 1850 census and disappeared by the 1870 census; hence the confusion about Dr. Kate's birth date, which is September 28, 1858.

An 1860 Kentucky census shows Stephen P. Berry, age 40, his wife Harriet, age 37, and three children; Alice, age 11, Claire, age 6, and Kate, age 2. This same census lists Mr. Berry as the owner of a woolen mill. His real estate was valued at $6,000 and his personal estate at $500.

Mr. Berry believed in education for girls. He sent them through high school. He was a man with ideas ahead of his time and, by being so, he did the world a large favor.

Stephen P. Berry, the sisters' father, took his family to Flatrock, Kentucky, before the Civil War. He bought a large piece of land and started a mill, which became a successful business. When talk of the Civil War was started he remained a Union man, while his neighbors all became secessionists. When war was declared, his neighbors all became Confederates and forced everybody to sign an oath of loyalty to the Confederacy.

Berry tacked a sign on his mill door saying he believed in the Union. A price was put on his head and he ran off to Ohio where he joined the Union Army. He stayed with them until the end of the war.

His neighbors took over his mill, planning to use it to grind grain for the Confederate Army. His wife Harriet believed in the

Union and, being a determined and brave woman, she went out to the mill at night, took out some basic parts that were needed to make the mill work, and buried them in the fields. The mill did not help the Confederate cause.

Berry came back from the Army owning nothing. His wife, Harriet, had died in 1861, so Stephen picked up his three girls and moved back to work in the oil fields of Pennsylvania. He remarried but was never again a successful businessman.

He put the three girls in school, but the middle child, Claire, ran off to get married and moved east. Alice and Kate finished school. Kate always looked to her older sister for advice and guidance.

Troost Hospital

When the Beltline Hospital closed in 1899 because Kansas City would not license a women's hospital, the sisters found a three-story hospital, run by women physicians, on the northwest corner of Eleventh and Troost Avenues. They rented larger quarters in this building. It had five free beds for poor children. There were many more requests from poor families than they could accept. They began to put two children in one bed, then three children in one bed.

The Troost hospital was for women, owned by women. This hospital also had all women doctors and nurses. This was not an accident; women were completely shunned as practicing doctors in early Kansas City, and they were forced to do everything necessary to run the hospital. This hospital had a two-year lease, but when the time was up, the hospital had to close.

This could have been the end of Mercy Hospital, but the positive and creative sisters placed the children in country and suburban Kansas City homes, where the doctors gave them medical and surgical attention. The nurses also traveled from house to house, caring for the ill children.

The people and newspapers of Kansas City martyred the women continually in these early years. As women they wept, but as martyrs they marched forward in search of money and supplies for the children in their care.

414 North Highland Avenue

In spite of the discouraging atmosphere, the sisters brought in the crippled children, cured them, and found homes for them, while charging the children and their parents nothing. They accomplished this feat without going into debt. They also had no surplus in the treasury. They had practiced rigid economy every day of the small hospital's life, but they could not continue without help. Getting a loan from a bank was impossible for any woman in 1897 or 1898. Alice, Kate, and the board held a conference. The only way for the beleaguered hospital to keep its doors open in Kansas City's hostile environment was to beg, so they begged, for the children's sake. This idea came from Dr. Richardson.

Many women and some men listened to them. The sisters had to prove themselves to the community before they could get help. They were seen as women first, then doctors, then contributing members of the community. There were no laws to help them, no belief in a woman's ability to produce outside the home in 1880's. The first group of people to pay for a bed was the young people's group of Kinsley, Kansas.

In order to care for the increasing number of ill children brought to them, the sisters began to send children to suburban homes and some to country houses. The Free Bed Fund paid for the children's expenses. Nurses took care of the children by traveling between the houses each day. The doctors also traveled between the various homes to care for the children.

The two women knew this situation could not last, and Dr. Richardson began to ask prominent businessmen for donations for a new and larger hospital. Dr. Alice Graham spoke to churches and other organizations, asking for funds for the new hospital. The response was good. The neighborhood church gave one of the first endowments for the children's hospital.

The sisters found an old home in a beautiful setting, overlooking the Missouri River. It was the Colonel R. H. Hunt home at 414 North Highland Avenue. Buying the house took all of the money available to them. They still had to make repairs and make it into a working hospital. The house became theirs on January 1, 1904.

They started making the necessary repairs, even though their treasury was practically empty. The 414 North Highland work depended on funds that were solicited daily. Dr. Richardson made the first payment and placed the hospital in the name of her sister, Dr. Alice Berry Graham. The two sisters remained in charge of the hospital.

MERCY HOSPITAL AT MISSOURI AND HIGHLAND AVENUES.

K. C. Star, May 9, 1909.

Kansas City Star May 9, 1909

The hospital then became an incorporated institution. The women did all of the work, but they were aided by building firms that gave wood, nails, and other necessary building material for their repairs. A drunken man and a woman helper laid the hardwood floors. Soapboxes took the place of chairs for eating meals by the furnace. Nurses slept in tiered beds, eight in a room. The old garages took the overflow. Tents were also set up in the yard to contain more children.

The children were moved into the new hospital as the work was going on. They came first; their care was considered a priority. This hospital also became a curiosity; visiting conventioneers were toured past the strange hospital to provide a comedic side to their visit to Kansas City.

The doctors put up banners on the trees to advertise the lowered child death rate in Kansas City. Dr. Kate had a sign put near the street letting the public know the needs of the hospital, such as twelve new sheets, twelve pillow cases, two dozen bath towels, and canned food. Several Kansas citizens and organizations stepped in to help the sisters at this point—Judge Slover, R. R. Brewster, and *The Kansas City Star,* to name a few. Others passed the word about their care for children, and more people began to help the beleaguered hospital. The ridicule lessened as time went on.

Their mortgage was small but had to be paid every month. From the first day of the new hospital, the working space was inadequate and every possible space was used for children.

Dr. Alice came down with cancer in 1908. She suffered for six years. Her sister and the nurses took care of her, but her suffering was great. This did not stop her work for the children of Mercy Hospital. She wrote articles, made phone calls from her bed, and dictated letters to Mrs. Carrie Volker and Mrs. John Wagner. She talked to heads of departments, solving the day-to-day problems of a children's hospital. She began writing a monthly article entitled, "The Mercy Messenger," often choosing the picture of a crippled child for it.

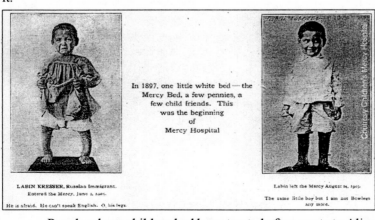

In 1897, one little white bed — the Mercy Bed, a few pennies, a few child friends. This was the beginning of Mercy Hospital

LABIN KRESSER, Russian Immigrant.
Entered the Mercy, June 2, 1903.
He is afraid. He can't speak English. O, his legs.

Labin left the Mercy August 14, 1903.
The same little boy but I am not Bowlegs any more.

Courtesy Children's Mercy Hospital

People whose children had been treated often wrote to Alice enclosing small amounts of money. She always accepted it because she felt their giving was necessary for their self-esteem as parents of cured children. The money helped other little patients.

R. R. Brewster became an important booster of the sisters. He was born in 1876 in Kansas. He graduated from law school in 1900. He worked for a law office in the same building as Alice and Kate. He didn't know the two women until one winter evening when both women were out and the doorbell rang. Brewster went to open the door. There he saw Alice with her hat blown to one side, her shawl blown from her shoulders and covered with snow. Later he learned that Alice had taken a child to the leased bed in the hospital and, not having enough money for bus fare, walked the many blocks home only to find she had lost her key.

Brewster started his own law office in 1918. He became a trial lawyer and took part in the scandalous Swope trial. Brewster became a good friend and advisor to the Berry sisters. He also became president of the Board of Trustees and attorney for the hospital. Brewster helped secure the home at 414 North Highland and campaigned for money to purchase it.

Doctors Graham and Richardson were shrewd businesswomen. They set up an all-women board called the Central Board. They knew how to delegate duties. This board handled the money given to Mercy, carried on the contacts with women's clubs, and set the rules for running the hospital schedules, all of which was so necessary for a smooth operation.

The Board of Trustees was comprised of five businessmen. They held all property in trust, and investment funds were given to the women of the Central Board. No one person owned the hospital. Women ran the hospital and worked in it to care for the poor crippled children of Kansas City and surrounding states.

The Women's Central Board had many responsibilities, including hiring personnel, approving medical staff, approving the budget, handling all details of repairs, and buying equipment. They handled all details of the hospital's six hundred clubs, such as the Kiwanis, Lions, and other clubs involved in giving to Mercy Hospital. They had one man who contacted the counties and courts about children who came to Mercy. He was a field representative who traveled over the very large area served by Mercy.

The hospital was expanding and needed more doctors. There were not many pediatric doctors at that time. Children who became

ill or crippled were treated as small adults. Women were in that cat-
egory also. Dr. Robert Shauffler became the first doctor to offer his
services at Mercy. He was a general surgeon who became an orthopedic surgeon for children. He worked without pay.

Dr. Shauffler became Mercy's first male doctor. He saw the
need for other doctors with various specialties and began to talk with
colleagues about giving time to the children of Mercy. The doctors
of Kansas City began to respond to the children's needs. They worked
one day a week without pay. With proper treatment, more children
could get well. Doctors Richardson and Graham welcomed the new
doctors. A dance club and a roller skating club funded two beds. In
addition, an artist sold baby pictures and gave the proceeds to Mercy
to help fund an annex.

The annex cost $175,000. This money came in small dona-
tions and took time to collect, but Doctors Richardson and Graham
did not intend to go into debt and risk closure of their hospital. The
annex was built onto the 414 North Highland house, adding much-
needed room to Mercy Hospital. The doctors proudly put one child
in one bed. They were in this hospital for fourteen years.

121 Clinton Place

Alice and Kate had very different personalities, but they got along together well and worked together for their hospital until Alice died, May 3, 1913.

After the first years of renting rooms in Kansas City, they discussed building a new house. They agreed on a piece of land at 121 Clinton Place. They talked to builders about the type of house they wanted. It had to have many windows for light and fresh air.

They furnished the house with heirlooms and furniture that Dr. Kate designed and built to fit in their home. Some of the men who gave meat to the hospital gave the whole calf, including the hide. The sisters had some of the hides processed and used them as rugs. They liked plain furnishings, but insisted they be in good taste. Both women liked flowers and enjoyed gardening. They wanted only the best plants, so they sent to Luther Burbank Gardens in California for white iris bulbs. There were also trumpet vines planted around the porch to entice hummingbirds.

Both ladies dressed in plain but well-designed clothing, their hair swept up on their heads in careful swirls, with every hair in place; this was quite a feat in those days before hair spray.

They also planted shrubs and vines around their hospitals. They felt that children needed beauty as much as adults. They used their house for themselves, ill children, visitors, and business. Their office was in the attic.

Mercy's Messenger

Dr. Alice started writing *Mercy's Messenger* when they moved to the 414 North Highland Hospital. It was a monthly publication, made of cardboard and was therefore sturdy, nine inches by five inches in size. It cost one and one-half cents for postage. She sent a different card every month to the people of Kansas City, giving news of Mercy Hospital and its accomplishments in health care of poor and crippled children. She encouraged those who had read the card to pass it on to their friends and families. The card also gave instructions to help recognize illnesses in their children. It encouraged parents to take a very ill child to the hospital rather than trying home remedies.

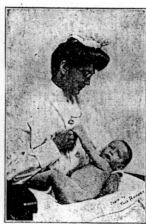

As John Oklahoma Entered The Mercy July 3rd.

As John Oklahoma Left The Mercy in April, Ten Months After.

DEAR MOTHER FROM A FOREIGN LAND:—
  The Mercy wants to help you cure your sick child and to help you to keep your well child from getting sick. Let us be STRANGERS no longer. Let us be FRIENDS. Visit the Hospital. Ask questions, that you may understand all that you see there. If you cannot come and yet need us, send us your address and we will go to you.
  All our beds are free and for those who cannot pay.

Visiting hours 2 to 5.—ALL DAYS. Out of town friends take notice. We Urge a Visit.

Mercy Hospital is NON-SECTARIAN. Its employees are required to abstain from all expressions which might in any way be contrary to the religious belief of any patron of this institution.
Visiting friends are earnestly requested to conform to this ruling.—CENTRAL BOARD

Mrs. Jim McClary,
Platt City Mo.

EXTRA

𝔐𝔢𝔯𝔠𝔶'𝔰 𝔐𝔢𝔰𝔰𝔢𝔫𝔤𝔢𝔯

Published by The Children's Mercy
Hospital

"The Hospital of the Little People."

Business Manager .... Bertha White

Editor for June, 1919.
Dr. Katharine B. Richardson
121 Clinton Place. Kansas City, Mo.

— 34 —

CHILDREN'S MERCY HOSPITAL—a
FREE NON-SECTARIAN, NON-LOCAL
INSTITUTION, situated at Independence
and Woodland Avenues, Kansas City, Mo.,
and devoted to the care of Sick and
Crippled Children.

On June 8 the Graduating Exercises of
Mercy Hospital's Training School will be
held at the Calvary Baptist Church, at
9th and Harrison Streets, commencing
at 7:30 p. m. Speaking by Mrs. Edwin
Fowler, Dr. Robt. J. Curdy and Rev.
Donald Munro. Music by the Choir and
by Margaret Fowler Forbes. General Re-
ception at the Hospital following the exercises. Come to Services and Recep-
tion. Mercy's friends are all invited.

Can Your Little Girl Walk?

OUR GRADUATING CLASS.

We said "War has decimated our
ranks." "Decimated" was good, and at
first it told the story, but later we
searched in vain for words to tell what
had happened to our Staff and Training
School. Dr. Francisco, Dr. Robinson, Dr.
Aull, Dr. Dennie, Dr. Bowman, Dr. Roberts, Dr. McCarty, Dr. Twyman, Dr. Hess
and Dr. Halberg all were quick to volun-
teer; and Miss Marvin, Miss Kelly, Miss
Scherenberg, Miss Rose, Miss Carney, Miss
Corbett, Miss Breed, Miss Mildred Headley, Miss Minnie Headley, Miss Friemonth
and Miss Welsh followed their brothers
across the sea.

But the nurses who stayed at Mercy
took up the doubled and trebled burdens
and were as heroic in their daily sacri-
fices as was Edith Cavell in the life and
death that have become illustrious. The
women who went out had the inspiration
of marching thousands all about them.
Theirs was the pride of sharing in great
accomplishments, the feeling that they
themselves were a part of something gi-
gantic, a movement in which they were
privileged to help strengthen and steady
the momentum of the world. But at
Mercy, the few whitecapped nurses wanting to go, and wanting to stay, feeling
themselves left farther and farther behind as the world moved forward, hearing every day the praises of their class-
mates who wore the Blue, with tears
they could not always control, with long-
ing they could not always smother,
turned back to the work that held them,
back to the fretful, irritating demands
of sick children, back to the silent lab-
oratories that held no physicians, the
deserted lobbies to which visitors seldom
came, and silently, nobly, lifted the bur-
den dropped from other shoulders, and
through four long years stood to prove
that there are many paths by which we
reach the heights of greatness.

Colored girls—nurse helpers—old men
—young boys — so-called "experienced
nurses," and women claiming neither experience nor training came at times to
help, and left always when they were
most needed. But the real nurses stayed
and worked and lifted, and now on
June 8, 1919, we come to publicly claim
our class of six as fit representatives of
the Mercy Hospital spirit and to pay
respect and honor to the Superintendent
and leader who brought them to their
fine accomplishment.

Mercy Hospital presents its little class
of War Graduates proudly and with confidence, knowing that no workers were
ever put to a severer test nor ever proved
more worthy of a title.

Don't offer some plan for us to carry
out. We already have more ideas than
we can put into practice. If you want
to help why just help. Don't suggest
extra work for the Hospital people. They
already have more than they can do.

Doesn't your love for your own make
you want to help others? It's a pretty
selfish love if it doesn't.

Courtesy Children's Mercy Hospital

The card always had a small picture of a sick or crippled child and sometimes a nurse taking care of that child. Even those who could not read could see the picture. This small card became a teaching tool for the mothers receiving them. One card had before and after operation pictures of a cleft palate patient.

The *Messenger* tried to meet the needs of immigrant mothers by having their message about Mercy printed in Italian and Yiddish as well as English. Dr. Alice asked a Rabbi and an Italian man to put the message into these two languages to help these women understand the message.

Dr. Alice stated hospital visiting hours; they were from two o'clock to five o'clock on all days of the week. She urged parents and friends to visit the children. One *Messenger* shows a nurse with a starved baby on her lap, then another picture of a healthy baby, after a stay and treatment at the hospital. In another card Dr. Alice reiterated that the hospital was non-sectarian, saying its employees were required to abstain from all expressions that might, in any way, be contrary to the religious belief of any patron of this institution. It added that visiting friends are earnestly requested to conform to this ruling as well.

In the early 1900's, Dr. Richardson discussed venereal disease in the *Mercy Messenger*. This subject was, at that time, considered to be completely undiscussable, anywhere or at any time. Venereal disease was a taboo subject in the home, much less in public. Of course, the *Messenger* belonged to the hospital. Dr. Richardson stated, "We will have to work with a thousand patients before we know more about these terrible diseases. The children suffer so much for the sins of their fathers." How she got away with that statement at that time is hard to understand.

A physician named Dr. Denny took care of these patients. He gave them sitz baths to relieve their pain. The venereal disease patients of all ages had their own ward and were not allowed out of it, nor could they have any contact with the other children on the fourth floor, where they stayed.

Ann's Pageant

Ann Peppard White wrote me several letters saying she had put on a pageant for Mercy Hospital in 1913. After an exchange of letters, we met. She must have been a dynamic lady in her youth; she was still interesting, but ill. She told me her story and her daughter, a nun, took down the conversation.

Ann lived in the west part of Kansas City in 1913, at which time she had just graduated from Kansas City Junior College. Girls of her day were thought to be well educated with two years of college. She had written a play while in school, and the students gave it for family and friends, with success.

Ann and some of her friends decided to put on the play as a summer pageant. The play was written around the verses of Omar Khayyam and the music of Lisa Lehman. The play was easy for amateurs to learn and present. Ann had brought home the script after graduation and, with friends, planned to put on the play in a neighbor's yard. While talking to her friends and telling how much fun they would have, they discussed the audience and how to get people to attend. They decided to do the play for charity, and everyone would hunt for a charity that would accept the money they made with their play.

Ann read *The Kansas City Star* one day and found an article asking for a leg brace. The little boy had had an operation on one leg and now needed money to buy a brace in order to walk. He was in the Children's Mercy Hospital on 414 North Highland Avenue, a small hospital in the north part of Kansas City. Ann had never heard of it, but she thought this would be an acceptable charity project. Her friends agreed. The brace would cost $200. Ann's friends were not too ambitious, but decided they could make that much money.

The first thing Ann had to do was to see Dr. Richardson to find out whether she was interested in their money. She called and made an appointment. The day arrived and Ann drove out to the hospital. She had the impression of a nice brown house and thought it to be Dr. Richardson's home as well as a hospital. The house was rather shabby. It did not have the feeling of a hospital, yet there were nurses and children in the rooms; some of the children were three in a bed.

Ann sat down facing Dr. Richardson. She suddenly realized she was talking to a dynamic woman who would make the necessary decisions. Ann explained her program, which had grown to include Lisa Lehman, an opera singer singing in the program, along with fortunetellers in tents and some dancers. Lisa Lehman was under contract to a New York agent and had to be paid for any work that she did. Ann explained to Dr. Richardson that, because Lisa wanted to help her friends, she would charge for her singing and then give the money back to the hospital.

Dr. Richardson began immediately, "Now I want you to know very well that we need the brace, but we have a special rule. I have made it and I intend to keep it. Anyone who wishes to give a benefit for us cannot in any way collect money for their own services or for their equipment."

Ann looked at her in surprise, because she didn't want any money out of the pageant. Dr. Richardson continued, "No I don't mean that you would take anything from it." Then she went on to explain about giving to Mercy Hospital. She had just had a small addition added to her hospital by the Bricklayers' Union. The bricklayers had given the bricks and their work as volunteers for the hospital. "I will never accept a dime which is not a pure gift."

Ann thought that was that. Dr. Richardson had just thrown the pageant back in her teeth, but she said, "Well, that suits us. We are not interested in charging for costumes and promotion or any of the rest of it. We will do what we can." After she left Mercy Hospital, Ann began to think about the woman she had just met. She was surprised at the doctor's vehemence because the paper of that time ran little stories about her, almost a short paragraph every week, saying Dr. Richardson needed something for some individual child. There were often some paragraphs that thanked people for their gifts, such as the ladies of Maryville, Missouri, who had sent two hundred jars of jelly, or perhaps ten jars. She thanked them saying, "We want you to know how much this meant to us, because otherwise so many children would not have had jelly on their tray."

There were little squibs in the paper saying, "We need sheets," or "Do you know we are making deformed children beautiful." Other

news articles explained that Dr. Richardson was anything but mas-
culine in appearance or manner, yet her hands had been trained to do
skilled surgery. They had taken on the strength that marked those of
her male associates on the staff of Mercy Hospital. The newspaper
was still trying to understand a female surgeon in 1913; it continued
to be a strange phenomenon in Kansas City.

After meeting Dr. Richardson in person, Ann knew another
side of her character. She now knew the doctor to be loving and kind
to the children and knew she would protect them with ferocity when
the occasion called for it.

The next morning R. R. Brewster called and said, "Ann, I
must see you tonight." That night Brewster came to her house and
told her to call the whole pageant off. He and Dr. Richardson had
thought about Lisa Lehman's plan to take money for her singing and
then give it back to the hospital. Dr. Richardson did not want any
under-the-table deals made in the name of Mercy Hospital. Mr.
Brewster and Ann continued to talk, both knowing Dr. Richardson
was right. R. R. Brewster still wanted the pageant for braces. After
much discussion, the pageant went on the planning board without
the big-name singer.

Ann and her friends began planning the pageant. They found
just the right yard for their production. A man named Mr. Dickey
had built a new home on a hill just across from the Nelson home.
Ann knew the Dickey boys and had eaten in their dining room, where
they could see the Nelson home across the valley. It was a beautiful
home, placed right across from the Nelson Art Gallery, on Forty-
fourth and Warwick. Ann asked for and received permission to present
the pageant in the Dickey lower lawn. It had a pool with beautiful
paintings around it and a terrace above. It made a natural stage.

The young people had a lot of fun organizing their pageant.
They had committees, headed by friends, who gathered the costumes
from neighboring attics: scarves, long skirts, and hats, as well as
spangled things for their hair. Some of the girls would play
fortunetellers in tents. They wanted an oriental look and told strange
fortunes because everybody knew everybody else. They charged a
good price.

Their group also had patrons who gave money to help set up
the pageant. Ann learned to be a promoter while she worked on the

theatre lights, led rehearsals, and organized time management.

Ann did have trouble with two wealthy ladies who decided to dance for the pageant. One wanted to do the new barefoot dancing that Isadora Duncan had introduced. That dance was acceptable, but the other wanted to do toe dancing, which Ann changed to a tap dance number. The lady was not happy and left in a huff.

The show was a success, though it did have at least one uneasy moment. The barefoot dancer came out on stage with a large Greek urn on her shoulder, and as she put it down gracefully, her skirt split open on the side, much to the delight of the audience.

The day after the pageant, Ann and her committee counted their money from the pageant. To their surprise, it came to $3000. Ann took the full amount to Dr. Richardson, who told her the board had decided to start a fund with this money. The parents could borrow from the fund and buy needed braces for their children. That way they would not be embarrassed by being given the brace for their child, and they could pay it back in small amounts.

Everyone had such a good time with the pageant in 1913 that when the next summer came, they decided to have another one. This time Ann talked to Lisa Lehman, who was again in town for the summer. Ann knew the opera singer was well known on the east coast, but not known in Kansas City. This time, in the summer of 1914, she explained that singing for a pageant would give Lisa some good publicity. Lisa spoke with her agent, who agreed to the publicity. Dr. Richardson agreed to allow the singer to perform in this second pageant.

Lisa Lehman had made a new record, putting tunes to nursery rhymes, and Ann suggested using this with children dressed in costumes and singing the songs from the record. The planning committee and singer agreed. The children came from the neighborhood and from the newly formed Campfire Girls, where Ann and some of the other young women had been working with the little girls.

The pageant included having children dressed in costumes of Peter Peter Pumpkin Eater, Miss Muffet, and a number of other nursery rhyme characters. The ladies learned that one of their friends could play the flute. They dressed him in a Pied Piper suit and had him stand in an aisle playing his flute while the children lined up behind him, coming from behind trees and bushes of the yard, and followed him to the stage where they sang the songs.

This pageant not only made the papers, but there were pictures of the child singers and a good write-up on Lisa Lehman. They also made a large amount of money and presented it to Dr. Richardson for the brace fund.

Mr. Loose Visits Dr. Richardson

Ann Peppard visited Dr. Richardson and wrote stories about Mercy's children for *The Kansas City Star*. The stories were printed, but Ann did not get paid for her work because women were not hired at the newspaper office. The stories of ill children made well by Mercy kept the hospital in the public eye.

Dr. Richardson told Ann the story of Mr. Loose on one of her visits, saying she could not publish it, but it was an interesting experience in Mercy's life.

Dr. Richardson said she received some attention from the big businessmen in Kansas City, and some of them gave money for her hospital. Sometimes the gentlemen tied strings to their giving that made their offered gifts impossible to accept. With this introduction, Dr. Richardson told Ann her story.

Mr. Loose started a bakery in Kansas City and his Zuzu crackers sold in five- and ten-cent packages. In fact, they sold so well that he enlarged his bakery and became a very wealthy man. He had a reputation of being friendly and kind.

One day he called Dr. Richardson and asked if he could come to see her. Dr. Richardson knew him only as a wealthy businessman, but said of course she would see him. He did not explain why he was visiting her, but they set the date.

When Mr. Loose came into her home he brought a young man with him, whom he introduced as his lawyer. They all sat down and Mr. Loose began the conversation by complimenting Dr. Richardson on her success with Mercy Hospital. He admired her good work with the poor and suffering children of Kansas City. He said he was sorry he had not come to talk with her before. During this flowery buildup she continued to hope he had come to give some money to her hospital.

He continued by telling her he understood it took a lot of money to run such a large organization. She answered vaguely, wondering what he was leading up to. He continued by repeating that he knew her work required a lot of money. Then he asked for her hospital budget figure for the year. She gave him an approximate answer.

Mr. Loose informed her he could manage that amount easily, and she told him she did not understand, still not saying no. She sat there, looking at this big pompous man, taking his measure, by this time in a not-altogether-friendly way.

The young lawyer spoke for the first time, explaining the situation. "Mr. Loose wants to take over your whole operation, the complete cost of Mercy Hospital. Of course he will change the name of the hospital and improve the care of the children. You will continue as the doctor in charge with a generous salary. The hospital would become The Jacob Loose Hospital."

Dr. Richardson started to speak, but Mr. Loose interrupted her saying, "You know, I could not only take over your budget, easily, on a yearly basis, but my wife and I have no children. We could give you papers, assuring you that our large property holdings would continue your operation after our deaths." The lawyer added, "The proposed hospital would then become a memorial to Mr. Loose and his wife."

At this point, Dr. Richardson got right out of her chair saying, "Memorial to whom? I don't understand. I would never change the name of Mercy Hospital. Why should I, for anyone? There are a great many people who have given to this hospital. I wouldn't have my own name on it, or my sister's, who gave her life for it. This hospital must continue as Mercy, as the peoples' hospital."

Mr. Loose quit smiling and said, "Well, Dr. Richardson, let me ask you how you are going to continue with this nickel and dime operation of raising money?"

In answer to this rude statement, she looked him straight in the eye and said, "Nickels and dimes! Isn't that how you made your fortune with Zuzu crackers? As I remember, they cost a nickel or a dime." After that statement, Mr. Loose and his lawyer left in a huff. She lost millions, but kept her hospital.

The sequel to this story is that many years later, Mr. Loose and his wife died and did leave a substantial sum of money to Mercy Hospital. However, Mr. Loose never could understand Dr. Richardson's philosophy, nor could she accept his.

The Independence and Woodland Hospital

The Highland Avenue residence had seemed such a large place in 1904, but the beds filled quickly. The sisters talked to some union men in the area, and they built an extra wing to the hospital, giving the materials and the work so the sisters did not have to collect money. Even then some of the nurses had to sleep in tents in the yard, much to the amusement of the citizens of the town. Children continued to come to the hospital until the beds had two or three children in them.

It became obvious to the sisters that a new and much larger hospital needed to be built. Their yearly budget came to $25,000. The question was, where would the money and property come from? Dr. Richardson spoke to her hospital boards about the need for a new and larger hospital. They agreed and began making plans. Mr. Brewster and other board members began to ask about property for sale and building prices. Kansas City was not a large city at that time, and word spread rapidly of their beginning plans.

Their property search ended quickly when Mr. Jenual Clinton Gates gave a two-acre piece of land at the corner of Woodland and Independence Avenues in memory of his daughter, Lulie. With that windfall, Dr. Richardson began organizing her helpers. They needed speakers all over Kansas City to let everyone know how much money was needed for a new and larger hospital. R. R. Brewster contacted building men to get an idea of how much money would be needed for the size of building they were planning. The men decided $200,000 would be enough to build an adequate children's hospital on the land they owned now.

Dr. Graham, although bedridden, wrote of the new hospital in her *Mercy's Messenger*. Collecting money became an all-out effort. The sisters discussed all plans before Dr. Richardson put their plan before the board. Dr. Alice died in 1913, two years before they started to build. The money for running Mercy had to be collected each year before they could collect for the new hospital. That amount of money was $25.00 a year per child; the children came first.

While collecting money, Mr. Brewster and Dr. Richardson

found a building contractor and carefully planned a hospital that would have plenty of light and fresh air in every ward. This was before air conditioning, so every ward had very large windows. There were also glass partitions between the wards and the hallways. The nurses needed to see the children from the hallways.

Finally, by 1915, the $200,000 had been collected. Mr. Brewster spoke at a victory meeting. He praised the board members, the businessmen, the church members, and some of Mercy's children for their hard work collecting money for the new hospital. He also mentioned the need to continue helping, or Mercy could not keep its doors open.

The carpenters had dug the basement and poured the concrete and some of the walls were started when they ran out of money. Dr. Richardson immediately called a halt to all building activities. She refused to borrow money to complete the hospital. She insisted Mercy Hospital should pay its way or it would not be built.

There was some argument with the board, but she had her way and everybody went into the money-collecting business again. Only when enough money was collected to finish the hospital did Dr. Richardson give permission to continue building.

When Mercy Hospital stood completed and ready for children in 1917, it was completely paid for; nothing was owed to anyone. Dr. Alice died two years before the new hospital was started, but Dr. Kate, who would always remember her sister, saw to it that the cornerstone mentioned Alice. The cornerstone inscription is this: "In 1897 Dr. Alice Berry Graham founded this hospital for sick and crippled children to be forever non-sectarian, non-local, and for those who cannot pay."

Mercy Hospital's new address became 1710 Independence Avenue. It stood ready to house the poor children of Kansas City and surrounding states. The new hospital had four floors, one flight of stairs, and two elevators. One elevator was for children and nurses, and the other was for freight, bringing the lunch carts to each floor, and moving beds up and down. It was a noisy contraption and had an unfinished look.

The first floor held the clinic at the Dykington entrance. It was a large room filled with long, wooden benches made much like church pews. There were examining rooms, therapy rooms, an x-ray

room, and so on down the long hall. Nurses and doctors came and
went among the patients, making it a busy place. At the Woodland
end of the first floor was the schoolroom and a large playroom with
a small pool for floating small boats. This room was used for Christmas parties and other parties through the year. The first floor also
contained the kitchen wing, which went back toward the playground.
Storerooms for the many goods given to the hospital were on this
floor as well.

The second floor had the receiving ward on the Dykington
Avenue side, plus a large ward with huge windows for children who
needed extra care after operations. The receiving ward had cubicles
to receive new patients after their thorough scrub with green soap,
after which the nurse popped a white gown over the child's head.
This was a new experience for many of the children who usually
took communal baths, once a week, in front of the kitchen stove for
warmth.

The business office was placed just inside the main door
facing Independence Avenue. This office dealt with parents and visitors, incoming and outgoing mail, and all the business of the hospital. The staff was all women. The Woodland wing of the second

floor had a big boys' ward named First East. It also had a ward of cubicles for very ill and dying children whose families could not take care of them. Dr. Kate had wanted this unit for a long time.

The second floor had a chapel with stained glass windows, one brought from 414 North Highland. This window had been moved three times. Mercy's clubs gave several stained glass windows to the chapel. The windows had names on them or non-religious poems. Parents and friends of the children could use the chapel as a quiet place to think and pray for loved ones.

The third floor on the Dykington side of the building held several wards for big girls. The large and small operating rooms were in the middle of the building, near the elevators. They were busy operating rooms, and the smell of ether permeated the rooms on that floor every morning. The big girls complained to no avail.

The third floor also had one large room used as a laboratory. Dr. Kate advertised for guinea pigs in the *Mercy's Messenger*, promising not to hurt them. That room too, was a busy place. All of the doctors had medical projects concerning children.

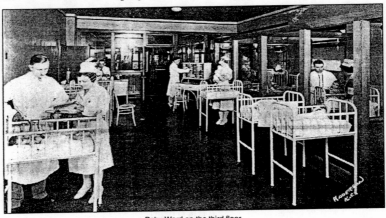

Baby Ward on the third floor

The isolation ward at the back of the building was a large area with big, glassed-in cubicles, each holding three to five children. Each room on that ward had its own white coat hanging by the door, ready for a nurse to put on as she entered the room. She washed her hands with soap and water before caring for the children. On leaving the room, she reversed the process. Dr. Richardson hated alcohol in all forms, including rubbing alcohol for cleaning hands, and did not allow its use in her hospital.

A large ward for babies on the Woodland side of the building held many cribs with one child to a crib. It also had a white rocking chair where crying babies could be rocked.

The fourth floor, at the top of the hospital, had interns' quarters on the Dykington side, and two interns lived in them. Both men were on twenty-hour call. There were no women interns. The interns' doors were always shut. Other than that, only the isolation ward doors could be kept shut. The fourth floor had fewer children than any other floor. A big ward for older girls faced the hallway to the sun porch and was filled with frame patients. That hall held the supervisor's office, with the light room on the other side of the clinic floor. Next to the girls' ward was a small ward filled with cribs for small girls with clubfoot. A separate cubicle usually held the very ill children with venereal disease.

Just across the hall was the ward for older boys spending the summer on frames. It was a noisy, happy ward; these boys were filled with hope for a bright future. The kitchen next to the boys' ward had a round table for walking patients, who ate their meals in the kitchen, whereas bed patients ate in the wards. The nurses kept a watchful eye on those who ate in the kitchen as they served the bed patients.

The new Mercy Hospital on 1710 Independence Avenue had all women in executive and nursing positions. Dr. Kate still paid her bills on time and did not buy new equipment until she had the money in hand. She bought only the best equipment for her children, and all of it had to be paid for. Dr. Richardson was a courageous and daring woman where her hospital was concerned. However, her plans for moving day for the children did not include asking for any help from Kansas City. She and her boards planned the time and day for moving. The old location of 414 North Highland was only two blocks away and across a ravine from the new hospital.

She sent home the children who could have a short home stay. She directed all the women and some men to line up in their cars in front of the Highland Hospital. This must have been quite a sight for the neighborhood. In 1917 not very many people owned cars, and men were usually the designated drivers. With drivers in line, nurses, doctors, and volunteers began carrying children to the vehicles. That car ride was a new experience for those sick children. They were carried into the new hospital and up the elevators, then tucked into bed. The elevator ride was also a first for many of the children.

Dr. Richardson and a group of nurses carried babies and walked from the old to the new hospital. A well-planned moving day was accomplished with care and dispatch.

The new Children's Mercy Hospital, 1710 Independence Avenue

Mercy's Children

The children arrived at Mercy Hospital's doors in many different ways. The first child was the abandoned little girl that Alice Graham brought in, when she walked on foot to their apartment carrying the ill and dirty child. Later the sisters carried clean children through the new hospital doors. Mothers, having learned of the hospital by word of mouth, came by streetcar carrying the babies and walking with older children. The children of the late 1800's who lived further away rode from their homes in horse-drawn wagons or carriages to meet the train to Kansas City. The mothers wrote to Mercy for acceptance. Fathers stayed home on the farm or on the job in small towns while mothers brought ill children to Mercy.

In 1897, division of labor for men and women made the children of a family the mother's total responsibility. Mothers took their children's care seriously. Some of the children came from orphanages and Juvenile Hall. Mercy's outworkers brought in many children.

One of the children, Arthur, came to Mercy from a long distance, brought by his sister. The other hospitals she tried would not accept Arthur. Mercy accepted him, and the sister worked as a nurse while he stayed there. Arthur had badly crippled legs that took a number of operations, and he had a long stay at Mercy. When Arthur finally began to walk, he was so happy about getting well that he sent for a friend who was more neglected and crippled than Arthur had ever been. Arthur assured his friend that Mercy could work miracles and he would get well, too. Mercy always tried.

Every child in the hospital had a spoonful of cod liver oil each morning. The nurse appeared in the ward after beds had been made, carrying a large tray with a bowl of cod liver oil mixed with a thick, dark molasses and rows of clean spoons. The children all groaned inwardly as she approached the first bed. Walking patients had to sit on the side of the bed while the process went on, and the no-talking rule prevailed. The nurse dipped a spoon into the thick mixture, twisted it around, and popped it into each child's mouth. She always waited until the child had swallowed the thick, gluey, dreadful mixture. Children had been known to wait until she had gone to the next bed, then they would hop into the bathroom and spit out their vitamin D. The reason for children taking cod liver oil had been carefully explained to the children. Dr. Richardson believed the children needed to know about treatments they were to be given ahead of time.

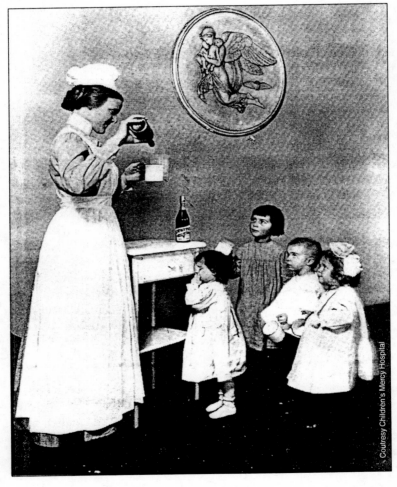

Courtesy Children's Mercy Hospital

After cod liver oil, the doctors began coming in. Each doctor had one visiting day a week and came dressed in a long, white coat. They looked very impressive to their young patients and the mothers who brought them. Many of them were there seeing a doctor for the first time.

The two interns were live-in and available at any time, day or night. The children looked forward to their doctor's visit and bragged that their doctor was better than the other visiting physicians. Sometimes the verbal battles became so vehement, the ward nurses had to step in and stop the battle. Everyone looked forward to his or her doctor's visit. Most of the physicians were bluff or smiling and friendly. A few were serious, but all were trying to help children get well. Everyone hoped to get good news about going home. Of course, this did not happen often.

As the nurses cleaned the wards, they talked to their patients, explaining hospital rules and treatments. They also explained about the doctors who hurried off without taking much time with a child. A dying child received extra attention so the others in that ward or floor knew a problem existed and were not surprised when a nurse came in to push that child's bed out of the room and down the hall to the elevator. The dying children were taken to a special ward in First East. No matter how noisy the wards had been, the sight of the departing child made everyone quiet, usually for the rest of the day.

The Mercy Hospital on Woodland had a schoolroom on one end of the first floor. Children who could walk or work their own wheelchairs went to school, taught by Mrs. Rollena Kearney in 1928. Walking children sat in desks or on a bench at the back of the schoolroom. This was where they did a group study such as learning or reciting poems for her. Wheelchair patients had boards fitted on the arms of their chairs to hold books and writing paper. An advantage to school, they thought, was that they had only one hour of the two-hour rest time after lunch. They played one-upmanship with that privilege and received lectures for doing so.

The constant training in being thankful for the hospital stays showed up in some Thanksgiving letters Miss Kearney had one class write. One child wrote, "I am thankful I am alive and well so I can go home. I am thankful that there is such a place as Mercy to come to. Also, I am thankful that such kind people are in this hospital. I am thankful I have a father and mother at home." Signed John. Another letter was short. "I am thankful that there is a Mercy hospital to come to and I am thankful that my legs are straight." Bertha.

Children in the wards reminded each other to be thankful, especially if a child fussed about the food or a nurse or doctor. They knew they were lucky, even when they were in pain or angry; they were there to get well. If they forgot, the nurses reminded them, gently, to be thankful for the care given by Mercy.

Some of the children stayed in Mercy for a very long time—as much as three years when having a series of operations. Their hair grew long, and barber and beauty students came to cut the children's hair for practice. They were taken to the first floor playroom where the students sat them on high stools, tied a cloth around their shoulders, and joked with them as they snipped away. Those student barbers must have been in the early stages of learning, for when they finished cutting the children's hair, it had a ragged-edged look, but it was shorter.

Dr. Richardson, when talking to the children on her visits to the various floors, gave the children hope. On these visits she followed her own orders and climbed the stairs, never using the elevator, many times carrying one of her babies who had cleft palate in her arms. Those babies were happy; none of them cried because Dr. Richardson had a way with children. One day she talked to Milton, who had a humped back. He told her he wanted to be a big, tall man with a wife and children someday. She told him she wanted those same things for him. He smiled, something he rarely did.

Mark had been a premature baby, but he grew to be an active child. One day he fell off the porch and was taken to Mercy Hospital. As the doctor stitched up Mark's scalp, he noticed the boy had a heart problem. A team of doctors took over, and he had an operation on his heart. Mark lived much longer because of the prompt treatment from Mercy's doctors.

One whole ward on fourth floor in 1928 contained children with clubfeet. They were five to eight years old. These children dragged themselves around the floor, using their hands to drag their legs. The nurses put them in wheel chairs, but the children preferred their own way of locomotion when the nurses were not looking. At home their families had made boards on roller skates to help them or pulled them in little wagons. Unless doctors could operate on their feet, the children would be crippled for life. The doctors of Mercy performed a series of operations, plus they made special shoes and braces for the children's legs and feet. It is surprising how little these small children fussed or cried. They were in pain a lot of their time in the hospital, but instead of crying they played in their wheelchairs or beds quite happily. They knew they were going to get well and walk. The doctors and nurses told them so every day.

Other children lived in full body casts or leg or arm casts for months. Those children were terribly uncomfortable, but they could laugh about their situation, play cards, and tell jokes, laughing uproariously with the other children. Quite often the nurses came in to quiet a ward that was getting too loud.

The big girls' ward on the fourth floor had eight frame patients. That must have been a nightmare for the probationer in charge of the ward. The teenagers could sit in a chair for the time the nurses made their beds, but they were not allowed to walk for the full three months of summer they spent in Mercy Hospital. They kidded each other about their summer vacation spent on Mercy's porch in the sun, calling it their private beach. All of those girls had to lie on their frames twenty-three hours each day, and some had buckets of sand at the head of their beds with a pulley and a chin strap. They wore this contraption as long as they could stand the pain, to help straighten their backs, but they didn't complain. These children had learned that their schoolmates made fun of them because their backs were misshapen. Toward the end of August, a bracemaker came in to measure the boys and girls for a new brace, to keep their backs straight for going to school.

Children on the fourth floor were not allowed to play on the floor and were lectured when they did. The few toys they had could be played with, one at a time, and then put away before meals or treatments. Other floors did allow children to sit on the floor to play jacks or board games.

Children with cleft palate were Dr. Richardson's patients. She operated on babies as young as one month old. She was a small woman, and the operating tools available to her were made for men and were too large for her small hands. Dr. Richardson, never at a loss for ideas, cut those overlarge operating tools down to her size. Her operations were works of art. The children with cleft palate were kept in Mercy until their operations and speech therapy were finished. This took several years to accomplish. Since a number of these patients came from other states, the children did not see their parents for a long time. The children accepted this long stay. The times they cried were when they received letters from home.

Dr. Richardson often spoke to groups of women about children with harelip. They were not liked or played with by other children and, if they were not operated on, it was believed that they would became criminals or go on welfare. People would not hire them for any but the worst work because they were so ugly. She enjoyed showing pictures of the children before their operations and after when they became pretty children.

One man who gave a substantial amount of money to Mercy was visiting the hospital one day. Dr. Richardson tried to hand him one of the babies with cleft palate and he refused to hold it. Dr. Kate said, "Shame on you," as she patted the ugly baby lovingly. A year later the same man came back to visit Mercy. Dr. Richardson came in to see him holding a nice-looking little boy. The man took the child and began to walk with him. Dr. Richardson laughed and told him it was the same child he had refused to take the year before.

During the polio epidemic, a group of thirteen- and fourteen-year-old boys and girls, whose parents kept them home to keep them from contracting polio, sent their savings to Mercy Hospital to help the children who had polio. One small boy decided the hospital needed a flag and gave one to be raised each day. He came to the hospital and raised the flag for them each morning for quite awhile. School children gave pennies through their schools. Children made gardens and gave the vegetables to the hospital. The girls helped their mothers can vegetables and make jellies and jams.

Two of Mercy's children came to the hospital in 1909; Little Bill, with pain in his eyes, was left dirty and crying on the hospital doorstep. There was no cure for the child, who sometimes screamed with pain all day, but on good days he played happily with his toys. Another child, Meredith, a beautiful little girl with tuberculosis, died. She had been found in a dirt heap; her parents could not be found. Dr. Richardson blamed these deaths on alcohol and bluntly stated her opinion of alcoholic parents.

When small purse mirrors were donated to the hospital, they were given to the older girls and boys to promote neatness. When

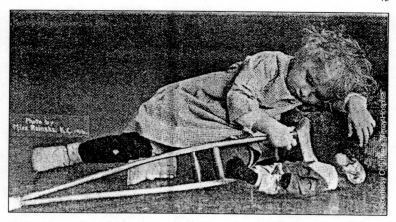

their beds were rolled out on the porch, they took their mirrors along. As they lay in the hot sun in their breechcloths, they shined the sun in each other's eyes and shrieked, "No fair!"

Miss Shirkey became Mercy Hospital's dietitian in the 1920's. She was a large, pink-cheeked woman who smiled at the children and discussed foods they liked. Her job was not easy. She had to balance the diets using the fruits, vegetables, and meats given that week or even that day. She solved the problems with serenity. Mercy's breakfast was toast and jelly, a bowl of oatmeal, and occasionally some fruit. Peanut butter and jelly on toast was considered a treat. Lunch included vegetables, meat, and a dessert. The evening meal included a vegetable soup and sandwich. Bean soup on Saturday night became a favorite meal of the week.

The big girls' ward on the fourth floor, in the 1930's, had a victrola and some records. They were dance records from the 1920's mixed with some opera records. The girls put on the records, wound the victrola, and listened. A few knew how to dance, but they were confined to their beds getting their backs straightened. Toys were few and far between, so the children had to be creative.

Eating habits varied from child to child. Some ate everything and asked for more, but some were finicky and wanted only one thing on their plates at a time. The nurses firmly believed children should eat everything on their plates. They checked the plates and encouraged those who did not eat everything. If a child refused to eat, the nurse sat down and fed that child until all of the food was eaten.

While talking to some churchwomen, Dr. Richardson got them to admit that when they were shopping for shoes, they sometimes did not like the six-dollar shoes and would buy those that cost ten dollars instead. She then told them to buy six-dollar shoes and give the money saved to a sick child. She also told the story of a family with six children. The father died of typhoid and the mother died a short time later, leaving the six young children alone. The five strong, healthy children were quickly adopted, but Mae had a crippling disease and was sent to Mercy Hospital. Dr. Richardson planned to heal Mae and to use the money her family left her to have her trained as the best secretary in Kansas City. Mae got well and, being a young child, was accepted into the orphanage.

One little girl had her legs cut off by a streetcar. The streetcar company decided they were not responsible and did not pay her anything. Mercy took her in, gave her artificial legs, and taught her to walk.

The summers were hot, and a hospital without air conditioning was stifling. Dr. Richardson sent some of the children to summer camps to keep them comfortable. One summer they were especially happy to have the camp arrangement because the city did not pick up the garbage for many days!

The Ill Children of Mercy Hospital

The ill children brought to Mercy came not only from Missouri, but from many surrounding states. Some of them came from Iowa, Nebraska, Oklahoma, and Arkansas. The children were poor, but were not all alike. The Kansas City children were street smart, with a large vocabulary of swear words, which the nurses discouraged. Some children came from small towns or farms and some from extremely religious communities. Being bright children, they shared their knowledge.

Marie came from a Kansas City Spanish immigrant home, and she had a large knowledge of Spanish swear words. She taught them to her ward mates. They picked up the words and meanings rapidly and used them. A new nurse came to the floor and understood what the children were saying and told the head nurse, Mrs. Smallwood, who took immediate action. The children of that ward received a stern lecture on acceptable language to be used in a hospital. The children stopped swearing in Spanish.

When a doctor decided to keep a child in the hospital, that child entered a whole new world. They were put into a large ladderback wooden wheelchair, allowed a swift good-bye to their mother's, and were pushed quickly away to the elevator.

Fathers were not found in the waiting room. It was mothers and women outworkers who brought the children to the hospital. The total division of labor made the mother the sole caretaker of the children. However, if they came by car, which was very unusual, the father's drove and left them off at the Dykington Avenue entrance, picking up the mother later. Women of the 1920's were not considered capable drivers.

The nurse pushed the child and wheelchair into the very slow-moving elevator; this was usually the child's first elevator ride. The ride was short because it was only one floor to the receiving ward, where the child received a bath and a white nightgown. Another ride in a wheelchair took the child down a hall and into a crib in a cubicle. The child could see and hear other children around them, but could not talk to them. The nurse gave the child her first instructions for living in a hospital. Be quiet, call a nurse if you need anything, and leave the crib side up. The child would be left alone. Those children usually joined the other children in crying; they were all very ill and away from home.

The children that Mercy kept either had problems their home doctors could not cure or they had never been to a doctor. In addition, there was pressure on the mothers to care for their children in their home. It took a daring mother to take her child to an out-of-town hospital. Small towns and country people could be very persuasive in keeping residents in line.

The small boy or girl left alone in bed surrounded by children calling "nurse, nurse" constantly was sometimes too frightened at first to call or join the never-ending chorus. However, they soon learned.

Dr. Kate believed in cleanliness and comfort for every child, which was something many of these children had not experienced. Their homes were heated with coal or wood stoves in winter. Most of them slept in unheated bedrooms. For summer cooling, they opened the doors and windows. A hospital with electricity, elevators, and telephones was a total culture shock for most of the children brought to Mercy.

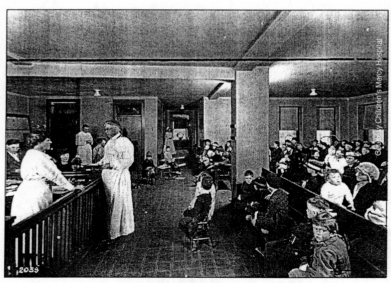

The waiting room was always crowded

The nurses, with their clean, starched, rustling uniforms, were kind, but they were busy caring for the children's health. They had little time to give to a homesick child. Many ill children were five and six years old by the time they entered the hospital. They stayed for two or three years, through a series of operations, and went home with special shoes and braces or in wheelchairs. They were brave children, but their bravery was born from the hope of walking instead of dragging themselves over the floor.

Other children had to live for months in a body, full leg, or arm cast. They were terribly uncomfortable, but they could joke about it. Some of the teenagers had a brand of black humor they used on each other when times got tough. The older patients wrote poems and played round-robin card games, passing the cards from bed to bed.

The boys and girls knew their backs were being straightened by spending all those hours strapped in their frames. Each frame was built specifically for each twisted back. Their doctor, usually Dr. Francisco or Dr. Shauffler, explained what he was trying to accomplish for them; those children listened to their every word. Some of

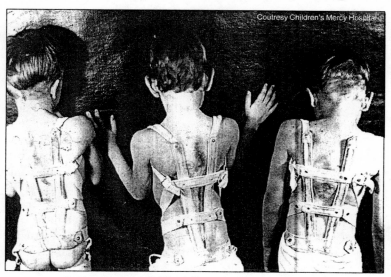

Coutresy Children's Mercy Hospital

Back braces for curvature of the spine invented at Children's Mercy Hospital the girls had a crush on their doctor and were teased unmercifully. Give-and-take in a closed society can be colorful.

At the end of summer, the frame patients went home to attend school. They wore body braces to keep their backs straight. The handsome young bracemaker came to the hospital to measure the boys and girls for new braces. There was a lot of joking and laughing as he measured and fitted the braces for them. They wore body braces to keep their backs straight while they were standing. Those older children explained to the younger ones what a crooked back meant to them. Other children had made fun of them and called them names, and they said,  in a serious way, that they found being an object of fun was not funny. They were willing to suffer frames and body braces for a straight back. Dr. Kate produced a number of small miracles in her unrelenting effort to have crippled children grow into self-respecting, producing adults, not public charges.

Dr. Richardson was everywhere. She often carried the babies with harelip as she went, telling all and sundry how beautiful they were. The poor little things, before their operations, were anything but beautiful, but Dr. Kate was seeing them as they would look after their series of operations. Performing surgery on the very young child did not become popular for a long time after her innovative work on children with harelip. It was around this time that the name for the malformation became cleft palate. The reason for keeping children so long was the long distances many of them had to travel and the lack of affordable transportation. Poor parents left those children for three or more years in the hospital because it took a series of operations to complete their treatment. Their parents missed those babies, who were being raised by the nurses. Dr. Richardson sent out constant reminders to the nurses about being stand-ins for trusting parents.

Wheatley-Provident Hospital

The sisters could not take African-American children into their white children's hospital. They tried numerous times by slipping a crippled black child in with the three babies in a crib, but they were always reprimanded by the nurses, parents, and visitors. Still, the black children needed care, and they were not receiving it anywhere else. The only answer was to have a hospital just for black children, staffed with black doctors and nurses. This was another insurmountable wall. There were black doctors in Kansas City in the early 1900's; they were segregated, but allowed to care for their own people. There were no pediatricians, but the children of the early 1900's were thought of as small adults and received treatment accordingly. Dr. Richardson began to look for a black doctor who might be interested in the care of small children.

She found Dr. J. E. Perry. He had started a sanitarium and nursing school for black people in 1910. It was a small building with eight beds and was operated as a proprietary institution until 1913.

Three nursing students were accepted in the school in 1911. Miss Mary Johnson graduated in 1912. One year of nurses' training sounds like a short time, but they were starting from zero.

After talking to Dr. Perry and getting his agreement to treat crippled children, Dr. Richardson began training a young black doctor in pediatric care. She also began talking to the Mercy Hospital doctors, who were giving their time to white children. She wanted them to train black doctors in pediatrics. These good doctors were reluctant, but she told them that although Kansas City did not have very many black doctors at all, there were none trained in childcare.

Dr. Richardson explained to the reluctant doctors that all ill children, no matter how poor they were or what their color was, deserved medical care. She lost her temper when trying to convince the good doctors to give their time and expertise to train black doctors. With her red hair and heightened color she must have been convincing, for some of the doctors relented and agreed to train black doctors in pediatrics.

Because Dr. Richardson was thorough in every undertaking, she realized the need of pediatric training for black nurses. She talked

CITIZENS' LEAGUE BULLETIN

To Popularize Civic Information and to Spiritualize Our Citizenship

No. 556   KANSAS CITY, MO., SATURDAY, OCT. 15, 1932   Non-Partisan

Mercy, "The Hospital of the Little People"

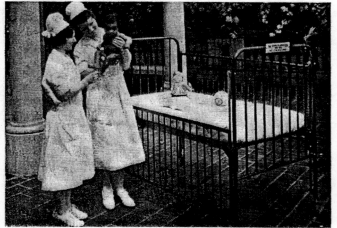

Mrs. Emma W. Robinson, of Olathe, Kansas, has, at "The Hospital of The Little People" endowed one lone little bed in which there shall be positively no color line. To this bed Negro surgeons and physicians may bring or send any little brown boy or girl who for some particular reason is beyond their skill or needs the unusual advantages that only a large hospital can give.

Courtesy Children's Mercy Hospital

some of Mercy's nurses into training black nurses. This project took great courage on Dr. Richardson's part as well as on the part of the doctors and nurses who agreed to take part in it. At that time the law of the land demanded segregation in both the black and white communities.

Still being thorough and mindful of Dr. Graham's dental care for children, Dr. Richardson found some black dentists who were willing to care for black children and who were willing to take extra training to do so. Nothing necessary for child healthcare was left out. Although Dr. Graham was ill with cancer by this time, both women began begging for poor black as well as white children. In this begging, the sisters were not left by themselves. A black civic group calling themselves "The Movement" organized and began to beg for black ill children. Their goal was to work with doctors to open the hospital as a free hospital for black people.

Dr. Richardson began adding to her begging speeches, asking for money to establish a hospital for black children. Dr. Graham added to this begging by writing letters to people of Kansas City from her bed, asking for money for both hospitals.

Some of the poor gave their pennies as well as substantial amounts of money to both hospitals; many schoolchildren also gave the contents of their piggy banks. A gentleman named Frank Niles gave Dr. Richardson a check for five thousand dollars as a first payment toward a new pediatric services building to be used exclusively for black children.

While speaking to various groups of women, Dr. Richardson spoke of the special treatments needed by black children. She earned respect from the people she spoke to, even when they did not like her personally. She was a tough lady who did not put up with fools gladly, or with those who did not agree with her. The problem was, she was right.

Another group, which called themselves "The Phyllis Wheatley Association," became active and helped raise funds for the proposed black children's hospital. This group was formed in 1914.

By 1916, enough money had been raised to build a two-story rough stone building at 1816 Forest Avenue. This building, called "The Model Ward," added twenty-five beds to the original eight-bed hospital. There was also a training school for black nurses.

A picture that accompanied the article announcing the opening of the addition to Phyllis-Provident Hospital shows Dr. Richardson and the prominent Kansas City physicians she had pushed into training black doctors in pediatrics. In this picture they are all smiling. Another picture in the same paper show three black doctors in 1924 receiving their pediatric certification from the twenty-month Wheatley Provident postgraduate program.

Behind this successful operation stood the Berry sisters. They had been so completely frustrated by the non-acceptance of crippled black children into Mercy Hospital that they came up with another way to care for them. Phyllis-Provident Hospital became an open door for black childcare. Black children needed care, and closed doors encouraged Allie and Kate to super-human effort. They and Dr. Perry plus many helpers, both black and white, had accomplished a miracle considering the segregation laws in 1913.

The Kansas City Board of Public Welfare had encouraged the two black organizations to work together for the new black hospital. It stayed open from 1916 to 1934, one year after Dr. Richardson's death.

Wheatley-Provident Hospital was owned and controlled by the black citizens of Kansas City, Missouri. It was the only institute of that nature owned by black people in the Middle West. They too operated on a shoestring, but they helped crippled black children and trained nurses for the Kansas City community, an amazing achievement for that time in history.

Before Wheatley hospital existed, black ill children were taken to City Hospital where they received poor and inadequate care. Wheatley filled a need for ill children.

Mercy's Clubs

Women began to form clubs to aid the ill children in Mercy Hospital. The first club formed in Kansas City was founded in 1904. The motto of this club was, "Let us all work together for good and do unto others as we would have others do unto us." Their song was, "Blessed Be The Tie That Binds." Doctors Graham and Richardson joined this club. They also visited other clubs to explain the hospital's needs and to praise the hard-working and devoted women club members. Their dues were five cents a meeting, later raised to ten cents, and even later to fifty cents. They stayed fifty cents until 1977 when, long after the founders' deaths, the dues became seven dollars a year.

When this club opened it was called The Union Aid Society. Later it changed to Maywood, its present name. For many years the Maywood club gave money to keep one bed in the hospital. In 1912 the club gave its money to Mercy, a ten-dollar check. They also gave a fresh egg shower for Easter. In later years they gave a tile floor for the roof garden and an Alpine Lamp. The club met twice a month. The Maywood club has grown over the years.

In its twenty-ninth year, The Maywood Club mentioned it had had twenty-nine presidents. In the 1920's three women appeared in *The Kansas City Star*. They wore very short hair and cloche hats. All were smiling. They were proud to be Mercy Club members.

Kansas and Independence had a number of these clubs. Two of the clubs were The Century Club and The League. The Century Club built and equipped a curative playground on the hospital grounds. They gave five thousand dollars in 1929 for this fund. The League held frequent rummage sales for the benefit of the hospital, but they had problems with their sales in 1920. Someone kept breaking in and stealing their stock before they could hold their sale. The newspaper reported these thefts and asked for help from people all over the city for more rummage to make the sale a success.

The sisters knew their ill children needed help if they were to get well. Knowing this fact, they reached out to the women who knew the positive side of having a well child. These women had been trained in homemaking skills, whether they lacked the reading and writing skills of their brothers or not. There were some schools, but many girls did not go to them. Some of the schools for girls gave a few basics in reading, writing, and arithmetic, but the girls of the eighteen hundreds and early nineteen hundreds also learned embroidery, dressmaking, and cooking.

The clubs working for Mercy were small neighborhood groups of women who made dresses and diapers for the hospital children. The hospital furnished all of the clothing for the children while they stayed in the hospital. Each morning a nurse brought in dresses for the girls, blue jeans and shirts for the boys, or gowns for those who were bedridden. The children in Mercy were used to a bath a week and one change of clothes a week. They complained bitterly about so much cleanliness: a bath every day—unheard of! The children's underwear was also handmade. The girls' had drawstrings in blue cotton cloth with legs to the knee, held in by elastic.

At one time there were as many as eight hundred clubs working for Mercy. These clubs were in Kansas City, Independence, and Missouri counties surrounding Kansas City, plus Oklahoma, Kansas, Iowa, Nebraska, and Arkansas. Women's clubs became a lifeline, keeping the hospital open against all odds. There were a lot of odds facing the sisters over the years. The women did not give up in the face of hardship.

The clubs started with the hospital at 414 North Highland. Some of them continue to this day. Some of the clubwomen in the present day are volunteers in the hospital, answering phones, reading to the children, pushing wheelchairs, or pulling wagons to treatment centers.

The Maywood Club, when it started, was made up of middle-class women who sewed for their families and kept backyard gardens to raise vegetables for their families. They grew fruit trees in their yards and canned all summer long so that their families could eat well all winter. Canning took many hours of hot, hard work. Children in the family snapped beans and peeled tomatoes for catsup. They made jelly and preserves, giving part of their canned goods to Mercy. They cooked on two-burner iron stoves that burned wood or coal oil.

The number of women in the Maywood Club climbed to

fifteen in 1912. They decided to stay at that number. These early members did not manage the family money; their husbands did. Many of those husbands did the family shopping, particularly farmers, and their wives never saw or spent any money. Women who worked outside the home had to turn their money over to their husbands and the men decided how much would be spent for the household needs.

The Maywood Club had several members of the McClure family in 1912. Mrs. McClure was president, her daughters were members, and Mrs. Nellie Stark and Mrs. Stark's daughter, Mrs. Charles Marker, made three generations giving their talents to Mercy's cause.

The five cents per month dues changed in 1913 to ten cents and again in 1917 to twenty-five cents. The hospital really depended on the money from the clubs. The summer when a number of the women went on long vacations, Mercy nearly closed its doors for lack of club dues payments.

The club amended its constitution in 1917, changing its name to "The Maywood Hospital Club." They also raised their dues to fifty cents a month.

Mercy hospital continued to grow, so the women branched out and began to give benefits, bridge parties, and dances to meet its extended needs. Maywood made an eight thousand dollar pledge for Mercy's "Wait awhile ward," which had its beginning when a bed was maintained for one dollar a day. They paid off the pledge in two years. In 1921 the club began paying expenses for the roof garden, giving two thousand dollars for a tile floor and enough to furnish some of the necessary fittings. This was in the hospital on Independence and Woodland Avenues. Later they gave an Alpine lamp and installed water coolers on every floor. They also paid for repairs on the things they gave to the hospital.

The early club met twice a month on the first and third Wednesdays. During their meetings they worked on sewing projects. After the nurses' hall was built, they met there.

The Maywood Club held a spring and fall rummage sale each year for a number of years. They also had a gift-wrapping bar at Woolf Brothers Store in Kansas City. It was a profitable project. Each year the club served at the antique shows. The proceeds of these many projects were given to Dr. Richardson at the installation luncheon, held in January each year. Three of the club's members, all past presidents, served on the Central Governing Board. They were Mrs. Karl Tickert, Mrs. Garret Walsh, and Mrs. J. T. Westwood, Jr. This club also had fund raising banquets for Mercy.

Times changed for the clubs as the years went on. They continued to work for Mercy. The amount of money grew and new food laws made the women stop giving home-canned food to the hospital.

In 1912, Mercy Hospital was declared the largest children's hospital in the United States. That same year, Dr. Richardson said that Mercy's death rate had been lower than that of any other children's hospital in the country. The clubwomen could be proud of their hospital.

One of the club's early members, a ninety-four-year-old woman, bought many yards of diaper materials, then hemmed them. She called them seat covers. These hemmed diapers were hard to dry before the days of automatic dryers.

The teachers of Kansas City who belonged to the clubs talked to their classes about the poor and ill children who needed many kinds of help. The school children responded by giving shows and plays to raise money for Mercy.

The Century Club was founded in 1922 in Independence, Missouri. This club earned money by holding benefit bridge parties and having concessions at the American Royal. They had a bottle fund and homemade bread sales. Most women baked bread for their families at least once a week. They had yeast that passed from mother to daughter. It made delicious sour dough bread and rolls.

The Century Club started with 100 members. Their goals were to be of service for Mercy Hospital and to be of help to sick and crippled children.

Dr. Richardson talked to the club often when it started. In 1932, the club members held an installation luncheon at the Meadow Lake Country Club to present the money their club had earned that year to the hospital. Mrs. W. C. Bowen, president of the Mercy Hospital Central Board, received $3,900 from Mrs. Frank Servatius. The retiring club president made the presentation. When Dr. Richardson talked to the clubs she gave them a report on the use of the previous year's check. She was meticulous in keeping the money straight and the clubs informed. She enjoyed joining the Maywood Club for theatre parties and concerts, though the clubs hesitated asking her because she was so busy.

The Century Club maintained the curative playground in the back of the hospital. Volunteers pulled weeds from the plantings around the hospital.

The League, another early club, answered Dr. Richardson's call in 1920 for a roof garden and sun porch on the fourth floor. This was to help tuberculosis patients. The project cost $5,000. She, of course, wanted the money immediately. It took awhile to collect, but she got it, eventually. Later they put an all-glass bay window on the fourth floor looking out on the sun porch. The bay window made a lovely sunny area in which to sit and read away from the hubbub of the ward.

The rules set by Dr. Richardson for the Mercy clubs were clear, concise, and to the point, even blunt:

1: Choose a few men and women who are all trying to, unselfishly, work for Mercy Hospital.

2: Don't be agitated about laws for a constitution. Don't copy the rules of any other organization. Such copies have gone through a dozen minute books already and are about as helpful as bumps on a log. Wait until you see the need, and then make the law.

3: Of course you will be told you can't start a club in a traditional way, but you can. Don't be in a hurry to make rules. They may work on paper, but will probably not be enforceable, or simply do harm.

4: When, however, a rule is accepted it will be either rescinded or the club will need to work for some defininte purpose, particularly as it pertains to Mercy.

5: Prepare the club's social life so that it may help and not retard the work planned. This is one of the most important and difficult undertakings.

6: The rules should not encourage unbridled social proceedings. Several of the Mercy's most promising groups have degenerated into a meaningless, pure social character. This had led to a gradual decrease of the leading membership.

7: If your club is maintained by dues, make the amount of these dues dignified. Five- or ten-cent dues are ridiculous and unworthy of the serious nature of the hospital. These rules were made during the depression, when many of the women did not have the five- or ten-cent dues to attend the meetings.

8: Remember, the good leaders arrange every detail of the club carefully; not to do so is to invite defeat. An officer, whose purpose is to set the object of each meeting, is no good. Choose your leaders after careful consideration.

Dr. Richardson had definite and carefully thought-out plans to help her successful clubs.

The club ladies made by hand the useful things hospitalized children needed. They made aprons, candy, pillowcases, and doll clothes for the bazaars they held for Mercy. These were resourceful women who also held dances and parties.

The clubwomen came in groups to tour the hospital to see what their work had accomplished. Men also came on these tours. They saw laughing children and crying children. These children were all clean, in their white beds that were changed every morning by a probationer. Some children were in wheelchairs, some walking in braces, and some playing group games like cards or board games. The clubwomen evidently liked what they saw because they returned to their meetings and continued their work. Each visitor had to put on a white coat when he or she entered the children's part of the hospital, to protect the children from germs.

The children in the wards stared back at the visitors and listened to the explanations being given to them. They did not always like what they heard. Some of the offended children stuck out their tongues or made faces at the visitors. This unmannerly activity from the patients always brought sharp lectures from the head nurse.

Experiences of Katherine Berry Richardson

Dykington Avenue was a rarely traveled street going past the west door of The Children's Mercy Hospital in 1923. The Kansas City Parks Department decided to improve the traffic flow in the north end of town by making Dykington Avenue an exit off Cliff Drive, therefore making the small street a well-traveled boulevard.

Dr. Richardson and her Board of Trustees, who presented alternative plans to improve traffic flow without using Dykington Avenue, immediately opposed this plan.

The Parks Department held a series of meetings on the street change. Dr. Richardson and her hospital friends regularly attended these meetings. They all tried to explain why Dykington Avenue would be a poor choice for a boulevard. This street ran by the west entrance of Mercy Hospital, which was the clinic entrance. Mothers and their children, some crippled, some healthy but taken along because there was no one to care for them at home, crossed the street to enter the clinic. A large well-traveled boulevard presented a dangerous place for the families trying to cross.

Mr. Scarret and Mr. McElroy of the Parks Department continued pushing for the new boulevard in spite of Mercy's explanations and alternative plans. Mr. McElroy owned most of the land in that area and offered to give enough to further the project.

An alternative way to exit Cliff Drive was suggested by a board member; this was through Highland Avenue, which would avoid the hospital entrance. The Park Board remained unconvinced and the meetings went on through the fall of 1923. The hospital board presented the fact that the number of mothers and children crossing Dykington in October was 3,147. Some of the mothers and children were outpatients walking long distances because they could not afford streetcar fare, which explains the large number. Mercy could not keep that many children.

R. R. Brewster and Dr. Richardson explained the hospital's inability to move the clinic to another entrance at one meeting. The explosive equipment in the clinic would be hard to move and the other hospital entrance was off busy Independence Avenue. Dr. Richardson, in another meeting, explained that Mercy had just bought land across Dykington for a future nursing home, making it even more important to keep traffic down on Dykington. She also hoped to get Dykington Avenue added to Mercy's property.

To prove her point, she invited the Park Board, with the exception of Mr. Scarrit and Mr. McElroy, to visit Mercy Hospital as her guests. She showed them around the grounds with explanations so they could see for themselves the necessity for a safe crossing at the clinic entrance.

During one of her presentations to the Park Board Dr. Richardson stated, "My twenty years of work has given me an abiding faith in men. In many respects, they are like children. They make the same kinds of mistakes children make, but when they are convinced of their errors, they are ready to correct them." Her board members and friends spoke eloquently for Mercy.

Finally, after a number of meetings, the bill for making Dykington Avenue a boulevard was defeated.

Dr. Richardson at one time wanted to buy the old Massey house and property for Mercy and also wanted to build a small hospital for black children. The neighbors rose up in anger and she had to give up her plan, not wanting to antagonize the people of Kansas City. The Massey home was on Jackson Street.

The first governing board was all women and for a long time remained all women. Dr. Richardson spent a lot of time explaining her actions while she ran the hospital. One of her rules was that no pulmonary tuberculosis patient was to be accepted in Mercy Hospital. Tuberculosis was very contagious and she did not want any child exposed to more disease.

She wrote a letter stating, "There is no greater work for these little ones than making over their tired, bent little bodies and strengthening their little feet to walk the roads of life."

The fourth floor sun porch had not only children and nurses on it, but pigeons roosted on top of the porch pillars. The nurses hated the pigeons and asked Dr. Richardson to get rid of them. Dr. Richardson liked the pigeons; she enjoyed walking out on the porch when no children were there to watch and listen to them. Also she believed birds should be treated kindly. The pigeons stayed on the porch nesting and cooing merrily and of course messing up beds. The nurses grumbled loudly while they changed messy beds on the porch. Nurses were also known to push some of the more agile boys up the posts to destroy pigeon eggs. The boys threw the eggs over the wires and sometimes dropped them on the kitchen workers peeling potatoes down below.

Dr. Kate's bright red hair turned white as the years went by, and she piled her curls high on her head. She was short but stood straight in her uniform. She wore a cape in cold weather, given to her by the hospital staff when the old one wore out. She did not buy anything for herself. Her time and money were spent on the sick children.

In the early years, when a child was dying, Mercy had no place to send them. They could not afford to keep them at Mercy where the space was needed for those children who could get well. This remained a problem for years.

Brady was one of the dying children who had nowhere to go. Brady had been picked up by one of the hospital's scouts. He had only a pair of overalls and no shirt, even in cold weather. His stepmother beat him with a broom until she injured his back. His father was an alcoholic who did not care about his children. The family lived near Colecamp, Missouri. Brady spent most of his days hiding in the woods. An older brother brought him food now and then, when he could.

When Brady arrived at Mercy Hospital they treated him, but he did not respond well. He was in constant pain that the doctors could not relieve. Still he learned to read and write and do arithmetic in less than a year after entering Mercy. He was a loving child who called Dr. Kate "mother." He never spoke badly of his parents, who treated him so cruelly. When it became apparent he would not get well, Dr. Kate took him home to care for him there. She cared for Brady until he died, and she buried him beside her sister.

No wonder she hated alcohol. She wrote on the subject: "In saloon days Mercy Hospital was not much more than a refuge, a receiving place for little victims of alcohol." She wrote this during prohibition.

A man named John Ivers got permission to ask what nationalities the children of Mercy Hospital represented in the early 1900's. He also got permission from the Board of Education to teach summer classes in Americanism. Ivers found Russians, Italians, Greeks, and Polish children, plus several other nationalities represented in the children he studied.

Like all the rules the sisters had made, the edict to accept children from birth to age sixteen was a definite rule that had to be followed. However, Dr. Richardson got around her own rule on a number of occasions. The parents of Viola Cutsinger lived far away from Mercy and wrote to the hospital asking them to take their daughter into the hospital. The girl was sixteen years old and had been in a wheelchair for three years. She also had a deformed hand. The family did not have the money to put her into a paying hospital. Dr. Richardson knew the girl would need a series of operations that would take more than a year. She had the parents' letter read to the Sunday school classes in Kansas City and suggested that the next Sunday's collection be given to Mercy for Viola's care. The churches followed through and Viola came to Mercy.

One Friday evening Dr. Richardson had only forty-five cents in the treasury. She went to the kitchen and talked to the kitchen manager. The manager checked the food in the pantry and asked Dr. Richardson what they were going to do with so many mouths to feed.

The two women began to search for enough food to last through the weekend. Dr. Richardson said, "A thousand times over the last fifteen years we have faced the same conditions, and our children have not gone hungry yet." Women had learned to stretch food during the depression years, making bread pudding with old bread, or putting more water in the soup.

One farm family in the mid 1900's, living near an Indian reservation in Oklahoma, had a bad year. The crops had failed and though the father shot prairie chickens and rabbits, the four children did not have enough to eat. One child, Dotty, was crippled. The mother had heard of Mercy Hospital from a visiting family. She decided to take the children to Mercy. She went to her trunk in the attic and took out her wedding dress and veil that she had brought with her from the coast. She sold it to one of the Indian girls who was to be married soon. She sold her hens and with the money she bought a train ticket to Kansas City. Children could ride free in those days. She washed her dress and the children's clothes for the trip. She wore her pale pink dress and stayed awake all night caring for her four ill children.

The family arrived in Kansas City hungry, having eaten all of their food the night before. The mother had one dollar left. She thought, "What if Mercy Hospital would not take them?" That thought could not be faced, so she asked the way to Mercy Hospital and found the streetcar to Mercy with friendly help from strangers. The conductor helped them on the car.

Mother and children arrived at the clinic door with the mother carrying Dotty. She had made no application in advance, and the four new patients would be a problem. Mercy was full, but Mercy Hospital did not turn them away.

The nurse in charge called Dr. Richardson. Dr. Richardson questioned the nurse for information on the family from Oklahoma. After hearing the nurse's answers she said, "They can't all be sick; I don't believe it. A woman in a calico dress, coming all that way. I tell you she just wants to get rid of her children. No application, no recommendation, from Oklahoma! Fill them up with breakfast and I will come to the hospital."

The nurses fed the family. Part of the children's illness was due to malnutrition, and the children stayed. This emergency was met.

Two of the children were well after two weeks, but Dotty needed an operation. Money was found for the mother, who needed to go home. Three of the children went with her. She was given money to buy back her chickens; the children needed the food.

The doctor found that Dotty, age three, could not live and the hospital sent a telegram to the parents to notify them. They also sent money to Oklahoma for the mother's trip to Kansas City. Dotty died with her mother beside her.

Now they needed a place to bury her. The mother could not afford a cemetery lot. They thought about putting her in the tiny space at Dr. Graham's feet. At the last moment, a friend of the hospital contributed a lot in Washington Cemetery that had been given to him in payment of a debt. Neither sister ever complained about any of these difficulties in their lives; they just went on solving the problems as they arose.

At one time the Board offered Dr. Richardson an $8,000-a-year salary. She refused to accept any pay for her work. She said, "If I can be hired, I can be fired, and I plan to work until I die."

Kansas City people who gave money to Mercy Hospital also found fault with its founder, asking why so many out-of-town children were accepted in the hospital. Dr. Richardson had an answer for them. "Come and see our books, and you will find that we have Mercy Hospital Clubs in more than three hundred places, scattered throughout the country. If it were not for the money that comes in from these out-of-town clubs, Mercy Hospital would have to close its doors."

Begging for Mercy Hospital

Begging for Mercy Hospital took many forms, and these forms changed as the hospital grew. The Berry sisters paid for the first bed to be used for one child.

As they found more and more crippled poor children, they realized the need for help. They had always lived frugally, paying their way and never going into debt. Begging for the needs of the children may have been hard for them at first, but knowing what they wanted for children made begging a necessity, and they did not hesitate once they started.

Those who offered help were hard to please. One of the first groups to pay for a bed was a group of union bricklayers. At first the bed was used for poor bricklayers' children only. One day another child was put in the bed. The union found out about it and told the doctors they would not pay for a bed if it were not reserved for bricklayers' families only.

Dr. Kate said, "No! The bed will go to the neediest child." The bricklayers union told her they would no longer pay for the bed. Then they thought about it for a while, held a meeting, and decided to give money for the bed, abiding by the doctor's rules.

Begging for Mercy did not go smoothly in another case. Churchwomen had been some of the first members of Mercy clubs. They also worked through their church groups to give money for the ill children. Ministers, nuns, and other clergy came to visit children from their congregations and were welcome on visiting days at the hospital.

One day, Dr. Richardson received a letter from the Ministerial Alliance informing her of their vote to give no more money to Mercy Hospital until it allowed Sunday School classes in the hospital. This was an unexpected blow to Mercy. The hospital did depend on the church's money.

Dr. Richardson immediately called a meeting of both her Boards, read the letter to them, and asked them why this was happening. The Board did not know and had heard nothing about any church trouble. Thoroughly mystified, they all went to their various homes in the city and called their ministers.

A few days later, the Board had another meeting. As it turned out, one of the big name and very popular ministers of Independence, Missouri, had visited a child from his church on visiting day at Mercy. He not only spoke with the child he knew, but busily gathered a group of children in the ward and began teaching them a Sunday School lesson. The ward nurse reported the minister's activity to her supervisor, who informed the minister of Mercy's rule. No teaching of religion was allowed in the hospital. This refusal by the hospital so incensed the minister that he called a meeting of the Ministerial Alliance. He told them his story and convinced the ministers of Kansas City and Independence to take punitive action against Mercy Hospital. They decided from then on, no church in Kansas City or Independence would help Mercy Hospital until they allowed Sunday School lessons to be taught in the hospital.

Dr. Richardson, good fighter that she was, met this new blow to Mercy head on. She called a meeting of both of her Boards and then called the Ministerial Alliance and invited them to meet with the hospital boards. The Ministerial Alliances came to the meeting, sure they would win Sunday School teaching in Mercy Hospital. They had the upper hand and the power to back up their threat to this uppity woman. Patriarchy was in ascendance in Kansas City, as it was in most of the country.

The powerful minister stood before the Mercy women and men, backed by the all male ministers. He stated his case and sat down. Dr. Richardson stood up, backed by her board members, and stated her case for Mercy Hospital. She explained the rule for Mercy Hospital, which had existed from its beginning. Because the hospital served children of all faiths, the hospital could not allow various faiths to teach its children without consulting others.

Dr. Richardson explained Mercy's rule by telling the ministers about the hospital's acceptance of Catholic, Protestant, Jewish, and Muslim children. She said she did not want anyone's feelings hurt. She reiterated the fact that the non-sectarian rule had been established since the beginning of the hospital. The ministers relented.

Dr. Kate wanted a laboratory in the new hospital on Independence Avenue. She wanted to have all the equipment for the study of measles, polio, and many other children's diseases that had no cures. She begged for a laboratory, but did not achieve it in her lifetime. However, being the strong woman she was, she did not give up. Because no large amounts of laboratory money came in, she established a very small laboratory in a large room on the third floor. She advertised in the newspaper for guinea pigs and rabbits, promising they would be well cared for. We can still find notes to Miss Anderson, the hospital supervisor, to please check the laboratory animals and make sure they were well fed, clean, and comfortable.

The doctors working at Mercy used this small laboratory. Children were often brought in to have blood tests. The doctors were trying to find causes for children's diseases they could not cure. The children were allowed petting privileges of rabbits and guinea pigs if they did not cry when the needle went in.

Another thing Dr. Kate needed was a place for dying children. She wanted the hospital beds for the ill children who had a chance to get well, but did not want to neglect those who were dying.

She asked for money for this project, but it took a long time to find an affordable place. A number of the hospital workers took these children home for kind and loving care until they died. The women of the families took care of them.

The Berry sisters hated alcohol. They joined The Women's Christian Temperance Union and worked for prohibition. They did not join a church, although they had been Episcopalian before coming to Kansas City. When prohibition became the law of the land, Dr. Richardson wrote on the subject: "In saloon days, Mercy Hospital was not much more than a refuge, a receiving place for the little victims of drink. Since prohibition, the hospital is a homelike place, in which paternal neglect and injury are extraordinarily rare and where the possible return of the past dreadful conditions were greatly feared." She wrote this in 1932 and mentioned that they had cared for 21,000 children that year. The year 1932 was a depression year. It was amazing she could beg enough money to care for that many children.

Dr. Richardson never told her age and never accepted any pay for the many hours she gave to the children of Mercy. She often said, "If you tell your age or accept money, they will want to retire you." She did not want to retire and never did.

Parents resented some of the strict rules of Mercy. One rule drew parental protest about food and toys the parents brought to Mercy for their children. The rule stated, "All food and toys brought to the hospital must be turned in at the office." Doctors and office workers then gave the food and gifts to children at Christmas and other holidays.

The year 1910 brought an unusually large money shortage to the hospital. Dr. Richardson asked the businessmen of Kansas City for permission to solicit employees of businesses and bank customers for money.

She received permission, and the program known as "Silver Tag" got started. *The Kansas City Star* helped recruit workers to solicit money for Mercy. The women wore a wide ribbon over one shoulder with a large silver tag and carried a box for money they collected. It became a yearly day of begging money for Mercy. The number of women who participated grew to seven hundred.

Eventually, people who were solicited while shopping and the people who worked in the stores who had given began to complain about the way the money was collected, and the Silver Tag Day came to an end. That year Mercy Hospital nearly closed its doors for lack of money.

Hospital costs reached their peak in 1927 when per-capita expenses reached two dollars and forty-five cents under a temporary superintendent. Miss Anderson, a nurse trained at Mercy, became the superintendent and per-capita costs went down to two dollars and five cents very quickly. That lady in her flowing silvery dress, high button gray shoes, and pince-nez missed nothing, and the hospital business began to run like a well-oiled machine.

She had help with the food. Miss Shirkey, a graduate dietitian, became the director in control of the entire food department. She knew how to manage good food on very little money. Food for the baby ward cost more than the nurses' table food, but none of it was too expensive. Each meal cost a fraction over seven cents per child, thanks to these two sharp women.

Dr. Graham and Dr. Henry talked to schoolchildren about kindness to animals and to poor and sick children. The schoolchildren gave the speakers a penny apiece for Mercy. Dr. Graham banked the pennies, one hundred fifty dollars of them, to be used by the hospital as an endowment fund.

The banks closed in 1929. This fund and many others were

lost. The banks opened later and paid three cents on the dollar; that was a blow to everyone.

All of the people collecting money for Mercy Hospital worked for no pay. Both Dr. Graham and Dr. Richardson brought large audiences when they spoke, and they spoke to people of many ages and stations in life. The washwomen were asked for nickels and dimes, hod carriers and drovers were asked for quarters, and white-collar workers were asked to give dollars.

Many people gave other gifts. One woman gave a bolt of cotton flannel for nightgowns to a club that made the gowns with the hospital's patterns.

One large gift of $10,000 was given in those early days, and Dr. Richardson hastily asked the clubs not to stop giving because of the large gift. She explained to her clubs that a number of people made pledges but took a long time to pay them.

Thanksgiving always brought large donations of food and money. The clubs set up calling committees for pledges. The car dealers lent cars to collect the promised goods and money. The cars covered the city, picking up donations. Kansas City Motor Dealers Association provided the cars. Women even went to the stockyards to collect money. Sororities held storytelling hours with Katherine Dunn-Hill from New Jersey. She entertained large numbers of children in the sorority members' homes, telling classic stories from Russia and England. The YMCA also had a storytelling hour for mothers and children.

Passing

The term "The Passing" seems to be unique to Mercy Hospital. It came about in 1928 when the Jaccard brothers asked Dr. Richardson for a charity they could give to Mercy in their mother's name. She suggested a supplementary food tray. The brothers, Walter M. and Ernest A. Jaccard, knew their mother had for years gone to the market to purchase fresh fruit to give, personally, to the Mercy children, so a food tray seemed to be a fitting gift to dedicate to their Mother. They gave $5,000 in her name. That was a lot of money in 1928. This practice of passing out food as a special treat became known as "The Passing."

The name "Passing" does not have any one author. It may have been a child who first called it that; no one knows, but in 1928 it became a routine part of a child's day in Mercy. When the Jaccard brothers had consulted Dr. Richardson about giving the money and its use, her idea evolved into a daily treat for the children.

Passing also became a time to remember birthdays. Some of the four- and five-year-olds could have a guest on the surgical floor at Passing time. Another Passing treat was a huge cake given to the hospital on President Roosevelt's birthday. There was enough cake for all four floors to enjoy.

Lunch at Mercy was early—11:00—followed by a two-hour naptime from 12:00 to 2:00. Not everyone slept, but they had to be quiet. Passing meant waking up from your nap to find a nurse with a basket on her arm, usually with a ribbon tied on the handle. The nurse passed out equal amounts of hard candy, fruit juice, or cake from a tray. The children all looked forward to Passing unless they were too sick to care. Some of the children did not like fruit juice, having never tasted it before. Sundays in the summer sometimes meant ice cream. The Sunday they put Grapenuts in the ice cream caused a loud cry of dislike from the children.

Some of the children grabbed their candy and stuffed it quickly in their mouths as though they were afraid someone would take it away from them. Others traded red candy for white or green. Cookies were also traded after the nurse left the ward. The children on foot were kept busy doing the trading from bed to bed.

Dr. Kate checked the Passing as she did everything about the hospital. When she found the ribbon on the basket frayed, or the cookies stale, she wrote a note to Miss Anderson, asking her to upgrade the Passing. She did not want it to be a second-rate treat.

Dr. Kate felt sick children needed a bright spot in their long days of shots, light treatments, or laying on a frame with a bucket of sand hooked to their chin straps. Many of the children were in pain after operations, but they could forget their pain for a few minutes when the Passing basket came by.

Candy was a rare treat for any of the children in the 1930's, and particularly for poor children. They were ecstatic on candy days. If a child ignored the candy, other children in the ward ate it for them, but they always asked first. Manners were important at Mercy Hospital, and politeness was strictly enforced by the nurses.

Doctors for Mercy

While the sisters were moving from one hospital to another, they had one doctor and one dentist for treating the children they found. After they bought the old house on 414 North Highland and remodeled it, they had many more children who needed different kinds of care. The sisters began discussing different doctors with various skills who might help them. They met Dr. Schauffler at one of their meetings and talked to him. He was a warm, kindly man who agreed to visit Mercy. He joined the sisters in treating the indigent children and stayed for thirty years. Dr. Schauffler became their scout for new doctors to join Mercy's staff.

Dr. John Aull came to Kansas City from Chicago, and Dr. Schauffler invited him to lunch and told him about Mercy's need for some of his time. Dr. Aull agreed that it sounded like a worthy cause. Dr. Schauffler then took Dr. Aull to meet Dr. Richardson and he joined the staff, not resigning until 1923.

Dr. Robert Schauffler was an orthopedic surgeon, a specialty that was badly needed for the many crooked backs and arms arriving at Mercy Hospital. Two more doctors joined the early staff. They were Dr. Scott P. Child and H. D. Jernowith, both internists. Dr. Schauffler and Dr. Richardson were looking for a well-rounded staff. These men had their own paying patients in other hospitals. They gave their time to Mercy free of charge. Many of them did not have special training in children's diseases, but learned as they treated the small patients who needed their trained skills in medicine. Dr. Richardson was the dominant doctor and remained so until she died. This state of affairs caused more than a little friction among some of the male doctors, who were not used to taking orders from a woman.

Another early doctor, Jesse E. Hunt, was a specialist in pediatrics. His specialty was infant feeding. Many infants died at that time because of little knowledge by the mothers about infant feeding. A lack of cleanliness caused most bottle-fed babies to die. Dr. Hunt joined the staff under the title of dietitian, later changed to pediatritian. He died at the young age of forty. The doctors did not always take care of their own health.

Dr. William P. Trimble became Mercy's first pathologist. Dr. Schauffler brought Dr. C. B. Francisco on staff, an outstanding orthopedic surgeon in Kansas City. Those two doctors worked together and came up with the frames for straightening curvature of the spine. They also worked on designs for the braces the girls and boys wore when they left the hospital.

The Mercy staff was given a room for research at the Hunt Avenue Hospital. These doctors wanted to make children well by using the best medicine Mercy could offer. They all had ideas that needed research.

In 1914, Dr. Virgil McCarty, who had just finished graduate work in Europe, joined the staff as an ear, nose, and throat specialist. Dr. Roberts joined the same year and these two men took out a lot of tonsils. Dr. Roberts resigned after four years and accepted a draft in service for WWII.

Dr. J. B. Cowherd became the head of pediatric service after Dr. Hunt's death in 1915. He, in turn, had to resign in 1924 to reduce his workload after a kidney removal.

Dr. Charles Denny joined Mercy in 1916. He became an efficient and energetic staff member. During his years at Mercy, he became a national authority on congenital syphilis. He remained very active for twenty years, then left most of his work to younger men, but during the war years he returned to the clinics. He brought some of his own office force to help the clinic work.

Dr. Harry Berger came on staff after Dr. Cowherd resigned. His specialty was anemia. He was an extremely active man. He got to the market early in the morning, went to the butcher shop where chickens were slaughtered for the Kosher trade, and collected pints of fresh chicken blood to take to the research room at Mercy so he could learn about anemia.

Dr. Hugh L. Dwyer came from New York to Mercy Hospital in 1928. Dr. Berger introduced him to Dr. Richardson. He started working at Mercy, doing research on throat cultures for diphtheria and vaginal smears for gonorrhea. Vaginal gonorrhea was a serious problem in babies in the 1920's. They blamed the problem on careless mothers. Dr. Dwyer resigned in 1938 to become Director of Health in Kansas City, Missouri.

Two dentists joined the staff in the early 1920's, Dr. Mont C. Carpenter and Dr. Fran E. Sheldon. They both remained on staff for thirty years.

There were a number of other doctors who gave their time to the children of Mercy. One was Sidny F. Pakula, who was an intern at Mercy in the 1920's. He gave time as a consultant after he retired. He was a popular pediatrician in Kansas for many years. His office was always crowded with mothers singing his praises for his care of their children.

Dr. John F. Stockwell did his intern work at the same time as Dr. Pakula. Dr. Stockwell was funny in a dry way. The children enjoyed watching him in action. Dr. Stockwell became a medical director of Mercy in later years.

Some of the doctors taught night classes for the nurses in training. They simplified their classes to help nurses understand the various diseases they must care for. The teachers also brought ill children to those classes, explaining the child's disease and the care required. The children listened avidly to the explanation of their diseases and went back to their wards with greater understanding than before.

In the early 1900's, the doctors wore long white coats to the ankles. These coats, which were worn at the clinics, were gathered at the waist. That style later changed, and the coats were made to hang from the shoulders with no tucks in the middle. The doctors' classes came to the wards to study the children, but their discussions were too profound for most of the children to understand. They were teaching in Latin.

There were other activities that the children understood better. They noticed that the interns and nurses did some kissing in the dark halls. Ill children took note of this activity and discussed it the next morning. Hospitals are interesting as well as busy places.

Dr. Richardson and
The Kansas City Star Newspaper

The *Kansas City Star* newspaper became a friend of the sisters as they continued with their campaign to help poor and crippled children. Their success became recognized and appreciated to some extent.

Dr. Richardson told her friend, Ann White, the following story of a visit to *The Kansas City Star* office. Dr. Richardson said, "I had a surprise telephone call the other day. It was from the editorial department of *The Kansas City Star*. The young man told me Colonel Nelson wanted to see me. I made an appointment, not knowing exactly what he wanted to see me about. The day of the appointment I felt quite excited. I had washed my hair, shined my shoes, and had chosen my best dress the night before. I was to be at his office by eleven o'clock. I had put on my hat and anchored it with two long hatpins in order to look my best, but my heart thumped with not knowing what I would be facing. To be honest, I was a little frightened. I took the streetcar downtown.

"Mr. Nelson was called 'The Barron' because he had tremendous power in Kansas City. He could be a great friend and a formidable enemy. I was ready to meet the challenge. On the second floor, I saw the editorial rooms were all in one open space. I learned later this arrangement of desks in an open space was Colonel Nelson's idea. He did not want any seclusion or meeting in the corridors. I thought the close desks and loud typewriters clattering away might make the editors' work difficult. I walked to the first desk and said I had an appointment with Colonel Nelson. I was taken across the floor by a young office boy. I had never been in the building before, but Colonel Nelson wanted to see me. He had published my articles for the hospital.

"In the corner of the room sat a very large desk with a huge man behind it. He had a small neck and a square face with sparse, white hair on his head. He looked straight at me with both of his large hands on the desk. The disciplined writers continued in complete chaos, to which the Colonel paid no attention.

"I can remember him sitting as though he would rise at any moment. I felt a certain amount of tension. He said, courteously, 'Young lady, sit down. I want to find out about you.'

"I looked him squarely in the eye and said, 'Yes.'

"He continued, 'You have been getting a lot of free publicity on your good works, and I want to know all about you.'

"Well, I got to my feet. I was mad; I didn't know whether I wanted to run away or not. I said, 'I can give you the facts from the very beginning from when I was born until I arrived in Kansas City, if you want them. Bring someone over here and have them write down what I tell you. If you don't believe me, send someone east to New York and check out my information.' I was still mad. I felt insulted, as if I had committed some sin of begging for the hospital.

"Mr. Nelson got very red in the face. I had heard of his volcanic temper, then he laughed and said, 'Now sit down young lady, that is exactly what I want.'

"I sat down, still seething, while he continued. 'You are receiving a great deal of attention through my paper with your begging. We want to know what happens to the things you are begging for. How do you run the hospital? Are you real or are you a phony?'

"I looked him in the eye and said, 'You will find out.' With that, he didn't laugh, but we became enemies. I didn't like being put on the grid, nor did I feel I had to explain Mercy Hospital to anybody. Yet I knew I needed *The Star* very badly. I sat there telling him about the education of my sister and me, the schools we attended and the dates we graduated, as well as the story of how we arrived in Kansas City. I told him how we had pinched and saved to come to Kansas City.

"I told him of our hanging out the shingle and not getting any business; then I told him how, after six months of waiting, my sister found a crying baby in a trash barrel. I described how she had brought it home, and that, I explained, was the start of Mercy Hospital. That first baby made us realize that there were children that needed us. We decided to take these poor children and manage some way. We used money we had saved and we rented a bed for that first child, but we soon realized we needed help to care for more children, so we started begging for these poor, ill children's care."

Colonel Nelson did send east for the sisters' credentials. He liked what he found and published the details in his paper. This helped the struggling hospital and the women who founded it. From then on, *The Kansas City Star* wrote stories of children who needed hospital care or a pair of shoes, or a dress, appealing to the community to give as they would to a poor relation, a part of the family. The little stories appealed to people, not only in Kansas City, but also to those in the surrounding counties and states, in a human, conversational way. Dr. Richardson may have made Colonel Nelson mad, but she raised his community conscience. He found the sisters to be real and dedicated women.

By the time Colonel Nelson called her to his office, Dr. Richardson was the head of a successful hospital. His greeting to her of "young lady" was insulting, as were his demands. When she answered him in kind, it must have been a shock to one of Kansas City's most powerful men. He did manage to accept her answers, but with difficulty. They were two people with quick tempers who worked for Kansas City's children. Dr. Richardson was never submissive.

Troy's Story

A short article in the newspaper mentions Miss Kearney, a teacher at Mercy. She taught one of the children who became a Mercy success in a number of ways. Troy Ruddick came to Mercy Hospital from Arkansas. He had a crippled hip and could not walk. Troy was fifteen years old when he entered Mercy. If they had allowed him to go home at age sixteen he could not have returned to Mercy, so he stayed for four years until he could walk out the door, cured.

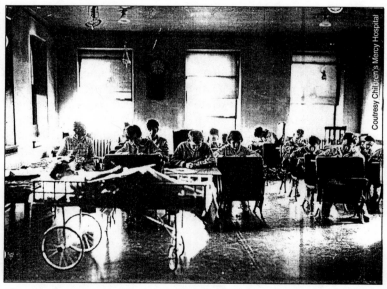

Courtesy Children's Mercy Hospital

Troy was an artist. He drew pencil sketches in art class in the schoolroom. Miss Kearney noticed how good they were. One day the talented police dog, Rin Tin Tin, came to the hospital to entertain the children. Entertainments were always held in the main entrance hall. All of the children who were able to move on their own or be moved came to see him. The second floor hallway was filled. This was a show in itself! The children came to watch in wheelchairs, on crutches, by walking, or they were pushed in cribs or wagons pulled by nurses. Children came from all floors. There were two elevators, one for children and one for freight. The people elevator was slow and smooth to ride in, and also had lights. The freight elevator was dark and it shook, rattled, and rolled, much to the children's delight. The children looked forward to these entertainments.

Troy went to the schoolroom the next day and drew a picture of Rin Tin Tin in pencil and gave it to Miss Kearney. She had it framed and hung it in the schoolroom. Troy continued sketching with pencil because school during the depression years did not have crayons or chalk for the students. One of the nurses bought him some oil paints. Those are messy and take room. That summer, since everybody spent part of their mornings taking regimented sunbaths on the porch, Troy was given the sunroom for painting.

Troy finished eighth grade in the schoolroom. Then Miss Kearney tutored him in high school courses until he could pass the tests and graduate from high school. He was a good artist and a nice kid. He always talked to the interested kids who came to the art room to inspect his work until a nurse would run them off. Someone was obviously showing Troy's paintings while he was still in the hospital because he won a scholarship for three years' study in the Kansas City Art Institute. After he left the hospital, able to walk, he attended the Art Institute, backed by the Young People's class of Trinity Methodist Episcopal Church. Everyone was glad that he continued his art education.

The Polio Epidemic

The polio epidemic came to Kansas City in the 1930's. The doctors had not dealt with this frightening disease before and could not cope with it. They did not know what germ was causing polio, and many children died. Those who lived were crippled, their families distraught. Ann Peppard had a friend, Martha, whose twelve-year-old brother was riding his pony one day and the next day was totally paralyzed with polio. His doctor did all he could for the child, but he remained extremely ill. Ann and Martha had grown up together and had been friends at school and scout camp together. Ann wanted to help her friend, who was extremely upset, and the boy's devastated family.

Physical therapy room

Ann suggested they go to see Dr. Richardson, who was by then recognized as an authority in the treatment of ill children in Kansas City. Martha agreed with Ann that an authority was needed for her brother. Ann called Dr. Richardson, who invited them to her house. She lived in a small cottage near Scarrit Point, so the young women drove to her home. Ann's description of the house is interesting. The room they were received in was a long, narrow front room with a large fireplace and lots of sunlight. Dr. Richardson met them and invited them in, had them sit down, and served them glasses of lemonade.

Martha explained what had happened to her brother and what their doctor was doing for him. It was a June day and the front room became very warm, so they moved out to the vine-covered porch, where they could get a breeze. The porch had several blooming vines, including a trumpet vine. In one corner Ann noticed a wren house and asked Dr. Richardson why she had a wren house so close to people.

Dr. Richardson said, "Well, Miss Peppard, you don't know much about wrens. They want to live next door to you. The same family of wrens and their grandchildren have come back every year since I have been here."

Ann asked, "You mean they come in through the vine and find their way to their own little apartment?"

Dr. Richardson answered, "They most certainly do, and you should hear them talking in the morning when their little ones come; it is quite a chatter. Oh they sing too, a sweet little song, like a sewing machine, with a lilt to it." They used treadle sewing machines at that time.

Dr. Richardson listened to Martha's story of her brother and absorbed the information. Finally, Martha asked whether her brother had a chance. Dr. Richardson answered Martha's question by saying, "Now Martha, your brother is going to get well. His doctors are doing everything right; believe that. Believe that he is going to get well because I believe it. I do not tell you it is all over. He will need you most when he begins to walk; he will need not sympathy, but strength. Watch him, help him, take him to the ocean to swim; water is a great healer. I do not mean to the country club where children are jumping all over and swimming well. But find a quiet place where he can gain strength and flexibility at his own speed. You have free time in the summer, give some of that to him when he needs you." Martha and Ann were in junior college at the time.

Martha's brother did make progress healing, though it was

slow, and by the next summer she took him to a friend's place in Maine where, with her help, the brother's health did improve. After a time he completely recovered. Ann said he went to school and became a businessman of Kansas City, married, and had children. This polio story had a happy ending thanks to Dr. Richardson's encouraging instructions and a sister's caring assistance.

Problem Solving

Aseries of misunderstandings took place at Mercy in 1916. A matron from the board of the First Baptist Church took two ill children from its nursery and brought them to Mercy Hospital. On arrival she demanded Dr. Richardson's personal attention. Dr. Richardson arrived on the scene, interviewed the matron and children, and did not accept the children into Mercy Hospital. The matron, Miss Dibble, took the children to St. Luke's, a paying hospital, where they were accepted as patients. Miss Dibble went back to church and told her story to her superior.

Dr. Richardson received an immediate phone call from the President of the Church Board. It seemed everyone at the church nursery had their feelings hurt by Dr. Richardson's refusal to accept the ill children. Dr. Richardson told him that the matron had been unreasonable when the rules of Mercy for accepting children were explained. These children's parents could pay for their care. She added they should send someone other than Miss Dibble with the next children from The First Baptist Church.

In 1923, a baby being operated on for cleft palate died from the ether. Dr. Richardson wrote to the parents explaining the situation. She stated that no blame could be placed on Mercy Hospital for the baby's death. Mercy agreed to take care of the child's body until they heard from the parents. This letter writing was the only way of reaching families who did not have telephones. The same poor families did not drive cars or have train fare for the trip to Kansas City.

The fear of contagion was always present, and parents and grandparents could be demanding. Everyone had to wear a white gown before entering the wards. One such case involved a father who demanded a visit to his son while the child was being prepared for a transfusion. The nurse assigned to the child, Miss Swon, told him he could not see the child until the transfusion was finished. The grandparents were there, and they demanded a visit to the child, right at that moment! Miss Swon refused their request. Dr. Richardson took responsibility for Miss Swon's decision, explaining the hospital rules governing operating room procedures, pointing out that Miss

Swon was following hospital rules.

Relatives of very ill children often became unmanageable in their demands. This group called Miss Swon dictatorial and arrogant. The child died. After his death came much discussion, and the parents finally agreed that Mercy had done all that could be done to save the child's life.

Dr. Richardson gave four-fifths of her time to Mercy Hospital. Only one-fifth of her time was given to her own patients who were in other hospitals. She kept her own patients separate because she charged them for her services. Some doors had opened for her.

Dr. Richardson received a letter thanking her for her attention to a child who had stayed in Mercy from 1904 to 1906. The parents thanked her for taking the child home with her every weekend to give her a break from the long hospital stay. This letter contained money for other children and expressed appreciation for her kindness.

Another case was much less pleasant. It involved a small boy with a broken leg from a car accident. His leg had been broken in several places. The doctor had reset the bones and had put the leg in splints. The father arrived the day after the leg had been set and demanded the child be released to him immediately. Miss Swon tried to explain the necessity of the child staying in the hospital until the leg healed. The father told her he had money and planned to take the child to a doctor in Oklahoma. Miss Swon, not sure of her authority in the face of the father's demands and promises, gave the child to his father. She sent an outworker to follow him. The father, once away from the hospital, unwrapped the bandages and splints from his son's leg and tried to make him walk. Then he took the child to a home in Kansas City.

The outworker went to the juvenile court and reported the mistreated child. Judge Porterfield continued to chew on his gum as he wrote out an order for the child's return to Mercy Hospital, where he had to start his treatment all over again. The nurses at Mercy not only had twelve-hour days of work, but when an emergency occurred they were required to work extra hours, without complaint. This time, they were glad to work extra hours to help this mistreated child to walk again.

Wages at Mercy were never high, but during the depression days of the late 1920's and the 1930's it became necessary to cut wages ten percent. But sickness took no vacation during those depression days; people continued bringing children to Mercy. In fact, there were more poor children than ever since the men could not find jobs as more and more businesses closed. The hospital had to send children home before they were completely recovered in order to care for the many very ill children being brought to them.

Dr. Richardson's secretary, Miss Lena Dagley, wrote thank-you notes for all of the gifts sent to the hospital. That in itself was a large job, for many people sent gifts of various sizes and kinds every day. Dr. Graham planned a larger "Messenger" to enhance Mercy's successes. She constantly worked for the hospital. She and Dr. Richardson took a trip to California to exchange information with another women's and children's hospital there. They found some things equal to Mercy, but many were inferior. They also visited several flower gardens and bought plants and bulbs for Mercy. Later they visited a hospital in Denver and several others in the East to exchange ideas on hospital care and management.

Due to ignorance at this time in history, many children died in dirt and pain. An outworker went to a home in Kansas City where a child had been reported to be very ill and dirty. The grandmother met the outworker and took her to see the ill child, who had flies on her and was visibly suffering. The outworker wanted to take the child to Mercy for care and cleanliness, but the grandmother said the child was much better off dying in her grandmother's loving care.

The Central Board in 1911 consisted of six people. They were as follows: Alice Berry Graham, President; Miss Carrie Bogel, Vice-President; Mrs. Minnie Hot, Treasurer; Mrs. C. C. Peters and Katherine Berry Richardson, Corresponding Secretaries.

The Advisory Board had more people, and a number of them were men in key positions to help Mercy Hospital deal with the city offices. These men and women formed the Advisory Board of Mercy Hospital in 1911: Judge H. L. McCune, Frank D. Crabbs, Reverand Charles More, J. E. Berbguener, Jacob Bilicoff, Edward E. Porterfield, Walter H. Holme, Miss Minnie Mutt, Louise W. Shouse, P. A. Simmons, and Walter Ruth.

A change in medical schools all over America had come in 1910. Many medical schools were closed because they were found to be inferior. A high-school education was now required for entry. This series of rulings closed medical doors to poor men, most women, and blacks. This change affected all hospitals and doctors for many years. In fact, only men with money could become doctors.

Mercy Hospital continued to grow in spite of its constant struggle to survive. Several things helped Mercy become a success: *The Kansas City Star*, its non-localism, its non-sectarianism, and its evident love of children, cleanliness, and good care.

Nursing History

In 1887, trained nurses did not have any legal standing in the state of Missouri or anywhere else. In fact, nursing was considered a woman's work. Many people looked down on nurses as second-class citizens in the 1800's, and families discouraged daughters from becoming nurses because they thought it was a demeaning occupation. By 1922, the state started a waiver system for nurses to practice if they moved to Missouri from another state. These waivers were based on experience. State licensing of nurses started in 1954. Recognition was slow in coming to the nursing profession in Missouri. Nursing licenses were based on tests given by state employees.

Nurses were first registered in Cape Colony, South Africa in 1897. In the United States, North Carolina began giving examinations and registering nurses in 1902, followed by New Jersey in 1904 and Virginia in 1914. By 1915 forty states began to formally register nurses. It took many years before nurses received state and national recognition for the care of ill people in homes and hospitals. Finally, hospitals recognized them as professional nurses. Good pay was even longer in arriving.

The first glimmer that nursing might someday be seen as a respectable profession began with Florence Nightingale during the Crimean War in the 1850s. She worked at nursing-profession training and upgrading all her life. She received belated praise, and a statue of her was erected in England after her death. The nurses following her had to fight their way up the nursing ladder toward respectability, step by step.

In 1904, *The Kansas City Star* mentioned a three-day training at Mercy Hospital. This was to be an informal update on pediatric training with discussions between doctors and nurses. However, the doctors planned to simplify the medical terms to help the nurses understand them. Both doctors and the newspaper of 1904 downgraded nurses in terms of mentality.

Until Florence Nightingale began recruiting middle- and upper-class women for nursing in the Crimean War, nurses came from the dregs of society. Nursing was connected with dirt, laziness, bad morals, and women of the lower class in English society. Florence Nightingale set high standards of cleanliness and care of the wounded men in the Crimean War. She had to fight for everything her nurses needed for the men's care. Doctors of that day were not aware of cleanliness as being necessary for patient's recovery. They fought her rules, but she persevered and won. There were some problems for the women; they were considered immoral if they were administering to men who were not part of their families, but with Florence Nightingale's leadership and training, nurses slowly became accepted. The fact that Florence came from one of the upper-class families of England did not hurt her cause.

When these nurses came home from the war, some of them worked in civilian hospitals. Trained nurses had problems being accepted into the English hospitals. Florence Nightingale's nurses' pledge was this:

"I solemnly pledge myself before God and presence of this assembly to pass my life in purity and to practice my profession faithfully.

I will abstain from whatever is deleterious and mischievous and will not take or knowingly administer any harmful drug.

I will do all in my power to maintain and elevate the standard of my profession and will hold in confidence all personal matters committed to my keeping and family affairs coming to my knowledge in the practice of my calling.

I will endeavor to aid the physician in his work and devote myself to the welfare of those committed to my care."

Nurses' pledges were based on this one. They changed as the years went by and according to the needs of the country that wrote the nurses' pledge. Each pledge writer added or subtracted from the original.

Nursing students from other hospitals came to study pediatrics at Mercy for four months of their two or three years of training. Training time for nurses also changed over the years. At Mercy, the students learned to keep the children's beds clean and white, with covers tucked in neatly, at all times. In early years, they were told they could not cry when caring for a very ill child. Such a large number broke down in tears that the rule was finally rescinded. It must have been a relief to those nursing students when they could cry over a very ill and suffering child.

From its beginning, the baby ward at Mercy had a white painted rocking chair in the ward. A nurse could sit down and rock a crying child any time she felt the baby needed tender, loving care. One day a new young doctor came in with a new theory. He believed that rocking spoiled young babies and that it wasn't necessary. One nurse continued to rock babies when she felt they needed it. She was punished by being sent to a teenage ward. She had always worked in the baby ward and was very unhappy, so she spoiled the teenagers. She brought in treats from outside, which was absolutely a forbidden practice for nurses. She was a supremely kind and loving woman. Eventually the "no rock" rule was changed, and the nurse went back to the baby ward to happily rock crying infants.

One of Dr. Richardson's statements, when she and her sisters were working on the nurses' pledge, speaks for itself. "Other nurses' training hospitals could hammer obey, obey, obey into their nurse's pledges, but I believe that shows a lack of respect for young nurses' by doctors."

Mercy's Nurses

Lena Dagley became Dr. Richardson's secretary while Dr. Graham was still alive. She was the one who sent advertisements to the newspaper asking for young women interested in nurses' training. The address on those advertisements was 21 Clinton Place, Kansas City, Missouri. They were sent from the attic office in the sisters' home.

The sisters' list of classes was long and inclusive. The regular course of lectures began October 1 and ended June 1. The classes and lectures were given by the Superintendent of the hospital and by staff physicians and surgeons. Special lecturers also came. There was a difference between Mercy's teaching and that of other hospitals; Mercy taught classes in dental care for children. They needed and got iron-willed women who could withstand the demanding hospital nurses' training.

A witty nurse wrote a prayer stating the proper nurse's outlook on her work.

> Now I get me up to work,
> I pray the Lord I may not shirk.
> If I should die before the night,
> I pray the Lord, my work's all right.

Mercy's nurses in 1898 had to endure, in silence, the ridicule heaped on them from the men and women of the community while they took care of the sick children who were being ignored by that same community. These nurses were dedicated beyond the call of duty. Doctors Graham and Richardson set the example for their nurses and other workers in the hospital. All of those women were convinced that loving care and hard work produced healthy children capable of becoming productive adults.

The sisters started training nurses with their first hospital. One reason they did this was because no pediatric nurses were available unless the sisters trained them. Both women had faced hardships all of their lives and knew that young women were bright, thinking human beings who were not afraid of hard work. Women of the 1890's were expected to marry when they were young, produce children, stay home to take care of them, and be subservient to their husbands. This did not appeal to all young women. The public ridiculed old maids, but not all girls wanted to marry young, and so many of those women applied for nurses' school.

Doctors Graham and Richardson decided the nurses' pledge of their school would be different. They noticed the patriarchal hospital nurses' pledges made it clear that the nurse had the duty of following the exact orders of the doctor. This left the nurse silent when the doctor made a mistake. The sisters thought women of knowledge had a right to protest when necessary.
This is Mercy's early pledge:

"I pledge myself to be loyal to all that is best in the profession of which I am a member. I pledge myself to strive to cooperate intelligently, conscientiously, and faithfully with the physician or surgeon in an effort to lessen disease and suffering, not by blind unreasoning obedience to orders, but through my realization of the dignity and responsibility of the nursing profession.

I will endeavor to do so, think and study and live that I may always act toward the sick with the sympathy of a sister and I will be especially mindful of the helplessness and need, by difference of race or creed or social position and I will hold before myself an ideal, not measured by money or personal favor or advancement, but that will always inspire me to give to my work the best of which I am capable."

The nurses had to memorize this pledge before graduation. The sisters believed that nurses had to think for themselves. This was a new concept for that time when most women were not allowed by law to think for themselves. The sisters had ideas that were advanced for their time, and they were in a position to act on them. Dr. Kate said, "A nurse is as important as the doctor, so she should be on the same level." This statement, by itself, was an unheard-of idea for the late 1800's. Dr. Kate said that three years of training were wasted on a nurse who did not think for herself.

The nurses in the sisters' first hospital earned very little money and sometimes were not paid; sometimes they worked for room and board. This was acceptable to the nurses, for they stayed with the sisters. When they moved from the Troost Hospital to 414 North Highland, Doctors Alice and Kate took applications and either conducted a personal interview with a secretary or candidates could send a photograph. Applicants had to be between the ages of eighteen and thirty and had to have a good education. This may have meant an eighth-grade education or a high-school diploma, or even a sixth-grade education. Girls usually did not go to high school in the 1800's.

The applicants had to be free of outside responsibilities and they could not be married. They had a probation of three months and were furnished with room and board. These students had to furnish their own uniforms. They were required to have three medium-blue–colored gingham dresses, ten long white aprons, six collars (Bishop style), and plain underwear—union suits were considered the best. The list continued: one wrapper, two laundry bags, clearly marked with the owner's name, a napkin ring, a watch with a second hand, and broad-toed shoes with rubber heels. The napkin ring was peculiar to the day. The union suit was a serviceable garment that protected the young nurses from the variations of heat and cold created by coal stoves and the air currents from loose windows and open doors.

The sisters were very particular in their requirements for the nurses' uniforms. Samples of blue gingham were sent on application with instructions for making the dresses. Most of the women of that time made clothing for their families, so this was not an unreasonable requirement. There were no stores carrying nurses' uniforms at that time. Some women could afford to hire seamstresses.

The dresses were made with perfectly plain shirtwaists sewn to the skirt back and sides, with two-inch box pleats sewn down the front of the waist. Sleeves must be tapered, ending in a band halfway between the elbow and wrist. The wristbands were long enough for a four-inch space at the back to be fastened with two white studs.

The skirt was slightly gored in the front and sides with a six-inch hem. The gingham had to be thoroughly shrunken before making the dress. That was good advice, because cotton material could shrink as much as an inch a yard in the early 1900's. The cotton material had to be ironed with very hot irons to remove all the wrinkles. The flat irons had to be heated on coal stoves. The iron handles made it necessary to use several hot pads to pick them up. Then the women had to iron first on paper or cloth to be sure the iron was clean and not too hot.

The aprons were to be made of very heavy bleached sheeting with a bib, slightly gored at the sides and front, and made the same length as the dress skirt. The apron had a six-inch hem. The bib pattern was furnished. Mercy's nurses had sturdy garments that were made to wear a long time, without showing the wear.

After three months of classes, probationers were permitted to wear the hospital cap. Dr. Richardson wrote to Florence Nightingale asking if she would design a cap for Mercy's nurses, and she did. The nurses signed a contract binding them to conform to all rules of the school and hospital for the remainder of the two years of training.

Probationers were to be paid eight dollars a month, and accepted nurses-in-training received ten dollars a month. These women had to buy their own textbooks, uniforms, and thermometers. Although they had to keep their uniforms in top condition, they were not allowed to use the hospital laundry. Back to the washboard for the student nurses! Thermometers in good condition had to be kept in the bib pocket of the apron at all times.

Student nurses took turns being present at sessions of the juvenile court. They were directed by the court or Head Nurse to attend to any case of outwork as may benefit the discharged patients or children under the care of the court. Their hours of duty were from 7:00 A.M. to 7:00 P.M. Some of their classes were in the evenings when doctors had time to teach them. Nurses were allowed two hours of that twelve-hour period to rest or study. They were allowed to have a half-day off each week from 2:00 P.M. to 9 P.M. and time to attend church on Sunday.

Once a year they had a two-week vacation, but time off for sickness had to be made up. Nurses and doctors gave the ill student nurses free care. There were several benefits, but the young women could be dismissed at any time. The incorporation of a training school for nurses started in 1901. It afforded the best opportunities to young women who desired to become members of an important modern profession.

The nurses at Mercy needed training in the care of adults as well as children to be well-rounded nurses. They joined a group of affiliated hospitals in Kansas City to get this training. The other hospitals sent their nurses to Mercy for pediatric training. Mercy's nurses were accepted in other hospitals as well as their own. The practice of thinking for themselves, which Doctors Richardson and Graham encouraged, must have been stifled as the student nurses continued their training at other area hospitals, all of which taught that nurses should only do what they were told by the doctors.

Dr. Alice Graham saw to it that Mercy had a dental department and training for the nurses in dental care and recognition of the need of it. After Dr. Graham's death, Lena Dagly, the doctor's personal secretary, sent letters of instruction to the would-be nursing students from 21 Clinton Place. In those letters, she made an odd explanation of what their studies would be like. "The course is general, not specific, and modifications will be made as the service of the hospital and education of the nurses demand. The course is severe, and those with sufficient health, education, and energy to undertake such requirements of the school and hospital should attempt the work." Many young women responded to the letter. The young women of that day who wanted to become professionals could choose to be teachers, nurses, librarians, or secretaries. The unrelenting regimen was a challenge to them. After the sisters drafted their nurses' pledge with its liberal statements, an art student, Beatrice Bennet, age 18, made four copies of it, framed them, and hung them in several prominent places in the hospital.

The other hospitals recognized the registered nurses when they graduated. Mercy's nurses were trained to care for children from birth to sixteen. Dr. Richardson felt the nurses trained at Mercy were a lot better off than those who went to China or Africa as missionaries. A number of young nurses were sent by their churches to foreign countries to care for children. Dr. Richardson explained the Mercy rules: "The hospital is non-local, non-sectarian, and devoted to the care of poor children."

Nurses' Hall

After the Woodland and Independence Avenue Hospital was built, Dr. Richardson knew her nurses needed a residence separate from the hospital. The new hospital had a wing for the nurses, but they were never away from their patients. They each needed quiet time and a room of their own. In her usual straightforward way, Dr. Richardson spoke to her hospital boards about a new nurses' home. They agreed with her and began planning to raise the money needed for land and a new building. They decided to speak to the men and women of Kansas City and those of surrounding states who had been helpful with the new hospital.

Courtesy Children's Mercy Hospital

They campaigned for several years, starting in the early 1920's. As always, Dr. Richardson would not start a building unless she knew she had all of the money to build a serviceable building for her nurses. Mrs. Joseph T. Byrd and her daughter, Mrs. Hall, gave two of the largest donations for the nurses' hall. This very interesting piece of news appeared in the newspaper as a squib on the back page of the paper. Women who gave large amounts of money to the nurses' hall were not terribly newsworthy.

They finally raised $170,000 from many sources and were ready to build. The city did not help an institution run by women. In fact, there was adverse criticism published in the paper from many of Kansas City's leading citizens. Why were they building a Nurses'

Hall when the ill children needed all the money the hospital could raise? Dr. Richardson did not start building until she had the whole amount necessary to finish the building. She knew that being in debt was not good for Mercy Hospital; a debt could shut down the whole operation. Nurses' Hall was built on a lot adjacent to the hospital, across Dykington Avenue. It was a red brick building to match Mercy Hospital and was finished in 1927. The Hall was designed to hold seventy-five nurses.

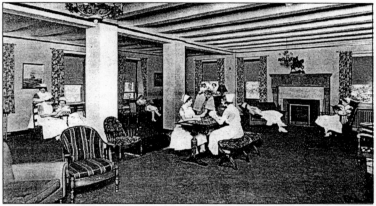

Mrs. W. C. Bowman, president of the hospital board, was happy to get the residence built, but she faced the problem of getting the hall furnished. The small amount of money left in the treasury was not enough to furnish this large building. But there were always helpers to turn to, and turn she did. The lounge was furnished as a memorial to John H. Berkshire. Mrs. G. N. Saurof of Cherrydale, Kansas, furnished the reading room as a memorial to her daughter. A few chairs and chests of drawers plus some other furniture were sent over from the hospital, but that was not enough to furnish 75 rooms for the nurses.

Dr. Richardson had some large old pieces of furniture she had brought to Kansas City from her family home. They needed repairs, so she talked to Ed Marcum, head carpenter of the hospital. He turned out to be a good furniture restorer. He took all the old pieces of originally good furniture and made them into beautiful and useable pieces for the incoming students and nurses. What furniture she did not have, Dr. Richardson advertised for in the paper. She asked for furniture made from cherry wood, walnut, and mahogany. She did not want cheap furniture that would not hold up. Only the best was good enough for Mercy's nurses. She stipulated that every room had to be different from the others, and they were. Dr. Richardson also restored some of the old furniture herself.

While putting the rooms together, Dr. Richardson asked for mirrors. She received enough mirrors to put one in every room. She had always insisted that the nurses have their hair combed and their collars straight. Dr. Richardson wanted her nurses neat and clean, so she also had large mirrors placed in the front hall of the recreation room. Mercy's nurses always had to check their hair and dresses before leaving for the hospital or for an evening out in Kansas City. These mirrors, like the furniture, had been given by the clubs and friends of Mercy. The residence also had housemothers who were chosen to keep the hall clean and in good order.

The Alpine Lamp

The sisters continuously searched medical journals to find new and improved treatments for Mercy's children. One article caught Dr. Richardson's eye. It told of an Alpine lamp being used to replace sun treatments for children with rickets. Dr. Richardson had great faith in sunlight and fresh air for ill children, but she had never used sun as a definite treatment.

The children with rickets had soft bones and were very thin. Many of them died. Some of those children came to Mercy Hospital and had been treated with varying success. The article said that one bed in a ward of "rickety" children was placed in front of an open sunny window and the child in that bed always quickly improved in health.

For a time it was considered to be a lucky bed. The doctors in the hospital began to watch the children in the sunny bed get well and began to study the effect of sunlight on other children. They discovered that sunlight had healing powers. Studies on rats proved the sun's rays through glass were ineffectual, but direct sunlight had healing ultra-violet rays.

Further studies found that a glass made of quartz would let ultra-violet rays through, and this finding led to an ultra-violet ray lamp with quartz glass. It was called an Alpine lamp. In 1903, Dr. Richardson read of a Dr. Rollier who had a farm in Leysin, Switzerland. He took a number of boys with various forms of tubercular infection and dressed them in breechcloths for maximum exposure to the sun and let them play outside all day. Many of the boys got well, but boys with tuberculosis did not respond to the sun treatment.

This is why all the children in Mercy wore breechcloths while on the porch in 1928. When Dr. Richardson read something she believed, she acted immediately. Her children began getting sunbaths, not just tuberculosis infection patients, but everybody. If sunlight cured one disease, it might cure others, so out to the sun porch went breechcloth-clad girls and boys to lie in the sun.

Not every day of the year was warm and sunny, so when the

Alpine lamp was invented, Dr. Richardson wanted one for her hospital. She called the Maywood Club and told them to start saving money for the lamp. They did as she requested. No one at Mercy knew anything about the lamp or how to use it. Dr. Richardson chose a bright, competent nurse who had been trained at Mercy to learn about the lamp and its use. She needed a woman with a technical background and scientific knowledge to understand the information the classes offered. Miss Vera Hall was chosen and was sent to an institution near Buffalo, New York for a year to become a specialist in handling the ultra-violet ray light.

Even then Dr. Richardson, always a perfectionist, continued her study of the light and found the best education in ultra-ray treatment could be gotten from Dr. Rollier in Switzerland. But where would she obtain the money to send Miss Hall overseas? Mercy Hospital was probably the most economically managed hospital in the world. Its patients were kept on two dollars a day, but it was always in need of more funds to carry on its care for the poor children.

At first Miss Hall was asked to save a part of her meager salary for the overseas trip, but Dr. Richardson soon realized that would take a long time. Always in need of money but never afraid to ask for it, Dr. Richardson thought of a man who had said he would not give money to the hospital, but he would donate funds for someone to study abroad. She talked to him and was able to send Miss Hall to study in Switzerland for a year. Dr. Richardson wanted a properly run lamp to let in the sun's rays and keep the children healthy.

Growing Older

D r. Richardson began to grow older. Her red hair turned white, but she continued to work. Her days were divided into two hours of work for her living, and the rest of the day was spent working for her hospital. One day in those later years she and a reporter stood across the street from the hospital talking of its future. She said, "Oh, how I hate to leave it."

The reporter asked, "Why, are you thinking of leaving Mercy Hospital?"

"I am forced to think strongly of it. Look at this white hair and thinning arms. Yes, I will soon be leaving Mercy Hospital. I have nothing I can bequeath it except the ideals and the spirit that I have tried to build into it. I want it to always be a hospital for poor children. I hope politics will never get within forty-nine million miles of it. The spirit I want to live on in Mercy Hospital is the spirit of true helpfulness and friendliness to the afflicted poor."

The year 1928 became a defining one for her. She fell at home, trying to wear some too-large slippers given to her by a friend. The fall caused a leg injury. She was diabetic by that time, and friends became worried about her safety while she lived alone. One boy whom she had taken into her home threatened her when she could not give him all the money he wanted. That too, was worrisome. Miss Anderson and some other friends and colleagues talked her into moving to Nurses' Hall. She went right on working, but everyone felt better about her because she was where they could keep an eye on her comings and goings, just in case she fell again or had other health problems.

Mrs. Haskel, who was a Board Member and a friend of the doctor, got a group of women together to visit Dr. Richardson. They went to Nurses' Hall, thinking she was retired, in bed, and ill. She wasn't well, but she was not in bed. In fact, when Mrs. Haskel, Mrs. White, and several others came to visit an invalid, they found her in the attic office answering letters. She was as aggressive as usual and talked of needing a new department in the hospital for the study of preventive medicine for children. She also mentioned the many dragons she needed to slay. One of the women asked, "What dragons need slaying?" Dr. Richardson told them infantile paralysis was a huge killer of children.

Her two-room apartment in Nurses' Hall was bright and well furnished. The women felt Dr. Richardson was being well looked after, even though she kept on working. All of her life, Kate had followed her father's often-repeated words, "The responsibility of an American extends beyond his own family. Wherever you go it is your duty to make good citizens of your neighbors." During those last three years, she wrote an article starting with, "When I die, what I leave behind me will be measured by the influence left on others' minds. Passing will not for a moment stop the wheels. If, my word, I could hold to my will those who come after me, I would not do it. There are only a few things that are fundamental, and if I have not been a force for perpetuation of those, then I have been a cipher. If I have been an influence for good, that good will live and myself, forgotten, will be my monument. How foolish to think anyone indispensable."

"Our work, yours and mine, is to hold Mercy Hospital to its very best, while we live to keep fully up with all that's decent to, somehow, some way, get a research laboratory for children's diseases to work as though we were going to stay here forever, and to realize that what is best will live on in the hearts of others and that, only so, shall we be monumented." Dr. Richardson died bravely and quickly, just the way she wanted to go.

Dr. Katherine Berry Richardson's Death

Dr. Kate died with her boots on, just as she had planned. She operated on Tuesday, May 30, dictated her correspondence on Thursday, June 1, became critically ill on Friday, June 2, and died Saturday, June 3, 1933. She had refused an operation to save her life and only accepted enough drugs to stop the pain. She remained a hero in life and death.

Her funeral service took place on June 7, in front of Nurses' Hall, under her favorite maple tree. All of Mercy's nurses were there in uniform, the graduates all in white with their white hats trimmed in black piping. The student nurses were there also, in their blue skirts, white aprons, and plain white caps. The Wheatley nurses, who also trained at Mercy, stood in a group wearing their nursing uniforms and hats.

Several Juvenile Court judges and the hospital supervisors and workers were there. The doctors came, plus many mothers with their small children and some of Mercy's patients. Another group attending her funeral were former patients, some with their mothers and some grown. One of the women attending Dr. Richardson's funeral was Mrs. R. G. Dwiggins, an elderly black women of Kansas City, Kansas. She represented "The Council of Negro Parent-Teacher Association." Mrs. Dwiggins brought a small crippled black girl to Mercy many years ago. Dr. Richardson accepted Marie Woods. That recurring story about a bed for the use of a black child was true, but difficult.

Marie Wood's wheelchair was given to Northeast High School for the use of crippled children attending that school. Mrs. Woods was there to represent her people who had been helped by Dr. Richardson. Dr. Burris A. Jenkins gave her eulogy. He was a very popular minister and speaker in Kansas City of the 1930's. He spoke eloquently of Dr. Richardson's love for children, but also mentioned the skeptical view she had of the world, while having an uncompromising spirit where the hospital was concerned. He ended with one of her favorite poems, Tennyson's, "Crossing the Bar." There were a thousand men, women, and children there in the square in front of the nursing home.

Dr. Harry Clayton Rogers gave a prayer and Miss M. Violet Fairchild sang, "Goin Home." Dr. Rogers also mentioned that black children, as well as white, called her blessed. She was buried in Mount Washington Cemetery in the W. C. Bowen lot. They decided to make a double grave and bury Alice Berry Graham with her sister. Dr. Richardson had never forgotten Alice and had always spoken of her as founder of Mercy Hospital. They both would have liked being together in death.

After the funeral, Miss Anna Anderson, Miss Hannah, Mrs. Bowman, and Mrs. Lena Dageley went back to Mercy Hospital and went back to work. Dr. Richardson would have approved of their care for ill children. Later a headstone was placed at the grave, giving the sisters' birth and death dates and one of their favorite poems:

> Others will sing a song,
> Others will right the wrong,
> Finish what I begin,
> And all I fail to win.

Both sisters read and liked poetry, and the inscription fit their way of thinking about Mercy Hospital.

Mercy Lives

Immediately after Dr. Richardson's death, her board met and issued orders to continue the hospital. Miss Lena Dagly became secretary of the board in place of Dr. Richardson. Miss Anderson remained superintendent of Mercy. After her came Miss Elizabeth Martin in 1937. When she retired in 1959, Miss Mary Hannah took her place. When Dr. Wayne Hart became medical director of Mercy, he contacted the University of Kansas Medical and Dental School and began working with them on children's illnesses. Doctors Kate and Alice were never allowed the privilege of networking with the male-run hospitals in the Kansas City area, except in exchange of nursing and medical students.

The hospital continued to treat patients free of charge until World War II. At that time, prices went so high, the governing board decided to accept pay or even partial payment from patients who could afford it. By that time a few of the patients had insurance on their children. The United States was just recovering from a long and tough depression. Dr. John F. Stockwell came back to Mercy and took the helm in 1959. He had been an intern at Mercy in the 1930's. From the day of Dr. Richardson's death, Mercy began to change. Dr. Hart became the Director, but the hospital still had many women in charge at that time. That too changed with time.

Mercy continued to care for ill children who could not pay. The doctors continued giving their time to their care. The women's clubs and Kansas City churches went right on working for Mercy's children.

The hospital on Woodland and Independence Avenues became too small for the many children who needed its help, as Kansas City continued to grow. The Board of Directors decided a new hospital should be built, so they started to raise funds for a new hospital. In 1970 a new and much larger Mercy Hospital was built on Hospital Hill at 2401 Gillham Road. The year 1970 came and almost went before the new hospital was ready for patients. However, the move took place in the middle of December. All of the children who were well enough to be sent home, went home for a short stay, leaving thirty-nine patients to make the move between hospitals.

They had a number of long blocks to traverse through Kansas City's busy streets carrying critically ill children. The new hospital put up a blackboard in its shining new hallway saying, "Operation Santa Claus." The children were carried or wheeled in the door; their name bands were checked and they were taken by new elevators to their designated rooms.

Kansas City responded to the move with ambulances for the incubator babies and the two burn patients on stretchers. This was not considered an emergency situation, but all vehicles carrying children were escorted with motorcycle patrolmen. Other patrolmen stood at corners with lights, ready to flip them to red, just in case of an emergency. The babies in incubators were each carried by six employees to an ambulance van with a generator to keep the power going to the incubators during the move.

A police captain stood on the old hospital steps explaining the process to a large group of people gathered to watch the move.

In the new hospital, Dr. Smull manned a two-way radio, keeping in touch with the old hospital during the move. The move went smoothly and they were finished by noon. Many changes had taken place in the 57 years between Mercy Hospital moves, but the very ill children were well cared for in each case. The new hospital in 1970 was a much larger building and had many more rooms with up-to-date equipment. Medicine had made many changes in the care of ill children, and Mercy continued to change also. Some things were brought from the old hospital and nursing home. Pieces of furniture that were refinished by Dr. Richardson still stand in hallways. There are mirrors in strategic spots; that was a must in Dr. Richardson's day, and it has carried over to the present day.

The public school continued to send teachers who went from room to room teaching the subjects the children were missing. One change in Mercy Hospital is the names on the administration lists. The Central Board in 1970 was made up of five men; the Governing Board had both men and women. Dr. Ned Smull, Director, and Dr. Richard Dregher, Executive Director, headed the administration list and so on down the line; all males, until one woman's name appears, Mrs. M. Dean Cowles, Director of Nursing. Dr. Richardson would have had one of her sharp remarks to say about so many men leaders and only one woman.

The new hospital is carrying on Dr. Kate's work and keeping the names of Dr. Alice Berry Graham and Dr. Katherine Berry Richardson alive as founders of the hospital. The sisters would be happy about the progress made in children's medicine. A school was named after Dr. Richardson, but no statue has been built in Kansas City to honor either her or her sister. Dr. Kate had been very definite that no statues or monuments be erected to them, and Kansas City has followed her wishes. Now, in the year 2004, Mercy has continued to grow, adding new offices and equipment as medicine adds new treatments for children's health. The waiting rooms are filled with children just as they were in the old hospital. One big difference is, now there are fathers as well as mothers waiting with their children.

Another change is the length of a child's stay in the hospital. It is hours, days, or weeks at the most. That is quite a difference from the days, weeks, and years of being in a hospital that the early children had to endure to get well. Mercy Hospital lives to make children well, and people go on giving to help the children.

Try a Greener Day:
My Series of Stays

in the Children's Mercy Hospital of Kansas City
when it was on Independence Avenue

by Bea Johns

Arriving at Mercy

My parents married in Warrensburg, Missouri, in 1919. I arrived June 17, 1920, a healthy, eight-pound child. My parents had a child every two years until I had two brothers and a sister. We lived in a three-room house, and things were a little crowded. Dad started an electrical business after reading through a shelf full of electrical encyclopedias. Mom had a two-year college education and had taught in Colorado, but after she had children, she stayed home with us.

In 1928, I became ill after a bout with whooping cough. All four of us had it, and my sister Joan and I had intestinal flu in the spring. Joan had a heart murmer from then on, and that is when all of my medical problems began.

Warrensburg is a college town, and in 1928 they had very few doctors and a small hospital. My health went downhill until a neighbor suggested Mercy Hospital in Kansas City. She told us they accepted charity patients between the ages of newborn and sixteen years.

Armed with this information and feeling quite desperate, my mother called our doctor, who confirmed the neighbor's recommendation and suggested we go immediately. He gave Mom a letter of recommendation for the hospital.

Dad had just started his own electric shop and could not leave town, but he gave us the old green pickup truck for the trip. Mom could not drive, so Uncle Harry took time away from his carpentry job to drive us to Kansas City. None of us had been there, even though it was only fifty miles away. They asked a policeman for directions, but he did not know the way to Mercy Hospital, nor did the second policeman. A filling station attendant gave us correct directions and we arrived at our destination, hot, tired, and late. The waiting room of the clinic had long wooden benches that looked like church pews. These were filled with wilted mothers and children of various ages. Babies cried, nurses dashed here and there. A nurse would come out to call a name and a mother and child would rise to take their turn with the examining doctor.

Mom spent a lot of time in the office, answering questions about our financial situation; we did not have one at the time. We were proven eligible as a charity family, if I had to stay. After the

examination, which was a very simple one, Dr. Berger told Mom that my hemoglobin registered twenty and I had to stay, adding that I would probably be dead in two weeks if I went home.

That settled the matter. A large nurse appeared with a monster, ladder-back, wooden wheelchair, and she put me in it. I waved goodbye to Mom as the nurse pushed me down the hall to the elevator. My first elevator ride took us up one floor, to Receiving Ward. The nurse proceeded to give me a bath with green soap and very hot water. I had just had a bath the night before; this seemed like too much cleanliness. We four children had one bath a week in the aluminum tub with the kittens playing around the old black coal stove. Our furniture was all early attic.

As my skin itched and drying hair began to stand straight out, the nurse put a long-sleeved, white cotton flannel gown over my head—this in June with the temperature 100 degrees in the shade. I thought longingly of the three sleeveless summer gowns Mom and Aunt Gladys had spent hours sewing the night before our trip. The nurse put me back in the wheelchair and pushed me down the hall into a room full of tiny glassed-in cubicles. She placed me in a crib, which seemed wrong to me because I was an eight-year-old girl! She neatly tucked me in and I protested, but got nowhere. Then she added the last insult to my dignity by pulling up the crib sides and locking it in place. She told me to be a good girl and left me in that small, dark cubicle. A baby in the cubicle across the aisle cried constantly under a pneumonia tent, while the long-snouted teakettle bubbled and boiled on the floor. Other children were monotonously calling, "Nurse, nurse," or crying. I joined them.

My First Days

Receiving Ward was a busy place. Soon another nurse came down the aisle with a large tray; she turned out to be a laboratory technician. She cheerfully took out a large, vicious-looking needle, talking merrily all the while. She asked me to hold out my hand, so I did and she punched a needle into my finger. She took blood until she could squeeze no more, then she tied a rubber tube around my arm and took a syringe of blood there. I began to think of vampire stories.

A long time went past, then a nurse with a basket on her arm came in. She rustled into the cubicle, talking to us and leaving a small handful of candy. This was my first experience with "Passing." I had missed lunch, so the candy tasted good. It was a good thing I had something to fortify me for the succession of interns, doctors, and nurses who came in to give me various tests for the rest of the afternoon.

Lights went out at 8:30. The nurse carefully raised the side of my crib. When she left, I slowly and quietly lowered it, hoping the nurse would not hear me. I must have gone to sleep because the next thing I knew a nurse was coaxing me back to bed and I was out in the hall by the nursing station.

After that walk, sleep proved impossible, so I lay listening to the many sounds of a hospital at night. Streetcars clanged in the street below and could be heard all over the hospital, the children called for the nurse, or they talked with each other. The nurse, when she did come, scolded the talkers, who hushed just long enough for her to leave the room.

I did not get any breakfast the next morning because, the nurse explained, I was going to x-ray. I did not understand the term "x-ray." Soon the heavy-wheelchair pusher came for me. We entered the x-ray room with its big black machine. The nurse and intern on duty began to reassure me; I must have looked as scared as I felt. The intern gave me a glass of chalky-looking fluid with green dots floating in it. The intern told me it tasted like milk, so I trustingly drank it. YUK! That was the end of trust. The machine did not hurt, but their effort to make me relax did not work because that table was cold.

Doctors came and went and I missed more meals, which was the least of my worries because I was never hungry. The technician came back for more blood every day. Finally, they decided I was anemic. With that, my stay in Receiving Ward ended and a nurse in a long blue skirt with a stiffly starched apron from neck to ankles put me in a wheelchair and took me on the elevator to the fourth floor. Part of the fourth floor, she told me, was used for interns' quarters, leaving four wards and one cubicle. After talking to the desk nurse, she wheeled me to a large, light ward filled with girls older than me. Although these girls had single beds, I found myself in a crib. The girls said hello to me and went on talking or singing popular songs. I listened quietly.

The next morning a nurse in a brown-striped skirt brought clothes for us, and we chose the things that looked our size. The dark blue underpants had drawstrings in the waist and legs. The ones I chose were too big and bagged far below my knees. The dress was not much better, but getting dressed after four days in a nightgown made the size an insignificant matter.

The brown-skirted nurse who was taking care of our ward that week told me I could get up and eat my meals in the kitchen. After days of tippy trays, this was welcome news. As we started down the hall, I asked a girl named Grace why all the nurses wore different uniforms. Grace pointed to the nurses as they passed us in the hall, each of them in a different-colored skirt and wearing a different-style cap. Miss Lane, who wore the plain blue skirt, was a Mercy probationer. The others came to Mercy for pediatric training from other hospitals all over the city. Grace also informed me of the rule against married student nurses.

We were the only girls at the table that morning. Grace introduced me to the boys just before the food was served, and we had to quiet down to eat, at the nurse's orders. When we got back to the ward I saw all the nurses pushing beds out of the wards, down the short hall, and out the door to a large porch. We stood aside as the beds went past. The procession included the children from ages one through seventeen. Their ailments included everything from cleft palate to bent backs. As the last bed went past, the nurse told us to go to our beds and get ready for our sunbaths. Grace led the way, and we found our beds on the other side of a screen drawn across the center of the porch between the boys' and girls' side. The screen preserved a semblance of modesty for the boys and girls. The nurses undressed the babies anywhere their beds landed. I climbed on my bed and looked blankly at the piece of cloth and string lying there. I watched the others tie the string around their waists and flip the cloth over it so they would get maximum sun. I did the same.

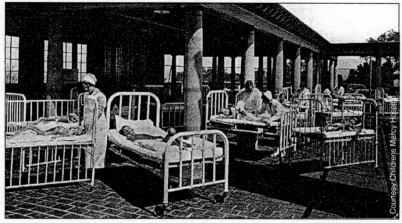

Miss Holloway, the assistant head nurse, held the watch to time our sunbaths, and at the end of fifteen minutes she called, "Turn over."

We all flipped over, but a nurse pushed my bed into the shade. The children still in the sun made envious remarks about those who couldn't take it.

Just then we heard ice tinkling in pitchers as three nurses walked out with carts of glasses and ice water. We could hardly wait our turn.

The big girls had brought small mirrors out, hidden under their pillows, and they amused themselves by reflecting the sun into the boys' eyes. The boys had come similarly equipped. When someone really got the sun in their eyes they either yelled with rage or giggled, until the nurses took away the mirrors.

Most of the children took an hour of sun, so by the time we were all in the shade and dressed, 11:30 and lunchtime had arrived. We ate on the porch from trays carried out by the five busy nurses. Our lunch had been sent up from the basement in a special cart and was cold. We had mashed potatoes, stewed tomatoes, peas with no seasoning, and bread and butter. Dessert was sandy Jell-O. The unseasoned food was good for me, but I wish I had known that at the time. The nurses stood in strategic places to see that we cleaned our plates.

I liked nap time on the porch. The pigeons sat on their nests or flew in and out, cooing as they went. Few of us slept the whole two hours, and the no-talking rule, plus the rule against getting up, made for a long two hours. The nurses hated the pigeons with reason because they made extra work. A hot battle raged between Dr. Richardson and the nurses. Dr. Richardson loved the big colorful birds and protected them; she enjoyed talking to them and would often feed the cooing birds when she came to the porch.

The porch had large, glazed brick that reached to about a child's shoulder height, then high black mesh, placed at an upward angle for about another four feet. In order to see over the side, we climbed up the wall by clinging to the wires and peered through the iron mesh. We could see the streetcars as they came rattling down Woodland Avenue, brakes screeching as they neared the corner.

About 4:30 in the afternoon our beds began to be pushed back into the building. At 5:00, Grace and I went to the kitchen for soup with bread and butter and a dessert of canned fruit. I decided I was going to like fourth floor. After supper, Grace and I walked out on the porch. Actually, Grace hopped. She had a short leg with a full cast, and she did not like wheelchairs, so she hopped. She said the wheelchairs were hard to push. A nurse called us to come take our baths. This was my first bath on the fourth floor, and the tub was so large, I could lie down in it. Grace bathed in the lavatory. For the first time since coming to Mercy, I went right to sleep.

A nurse with a tray came into the ward just after we were cleaned up for the morning and sat a tray on my stand. She then took a spoon from the many precisely arranged on the tray. She carefully dipped the spoon into a bowl of dark, thick syrup, gave it a deft twist to keep the blob in place, and popped it into my mouth. That cod liver oil was hard to swallow. I grabbed my glass of water and drank frantically; the oil went down, but the taste lingered.

Each child on the fourth floor received a spoonful of cod liver oil every morning. Some of the older girls tried to hold it in their mouths, not swallowing, but the nurse stood there, firmly insisting on their downing the oil before she moved to the next bed.

A few weeks in the sun made me the second brownest child on the porch. The brownest was Earnest, a three-year-old who had tuberculosis of the spine. He had lived for a short time in an orphanage just behind the hospital, but most of his life had been spent in an iron frame, with pads at strategic places to keep his back straight. He always had a belt buckled firmly around his pudgy middle to keep him in place. He kicked his legs high in the air and waved his arms constantly. Since hospital meant home to him, he was a happy boy and laughed with the nurses.

Grace became my special friend over the next five years. She had tuberculosis and had one good leg. Her short leg was in a cast from the waist to ankle, but she rarely complained. She had short, ragged brown hair. I learned the reason for that one day when we went down to the playroom on the first floor, where the barber students cut our hair.

In our ward of eight girls, Grace and I were the only ones who could get out of bed officially. The other girls were frame patients and were never allowed to get out of bed or even to sit up. They had curvature of the spine and had been coming to the hospital every summer for a number of years. They teased each other about their pleasant stay at the Mercy Summer Resort, complete with sun bathing and bedpans. One girl named Katie made a poster to advertise our invigorating air and superb peanut butter sandwiches. She hung it over her bed, but the ward nurse made her take it down before inspection.

Inspections

Inspection took place every morning after beds were made up by the ward nurse. One nurse had more than she could do in our ward to change the beds with those heavy frames in place, so Grace and I were pressed into service. I learned to carry bedpans and emesis basins for tooth brushing, and how to make beds. Grace and I became so good with envelope corners that our beds always passed inspection. Until I carried bedpans, I had not given much thought to a future career, but after that experience I decided not to be a nurse.

Martha was an artist who spent her time drawing pictures with stubs of crayons given to her by the nurses when they swept them up. She did her drawing while lying flat on her back. Barbara in the next bed pulled her chin strap, which was weighted with a bucket of sand, fitted it carefully over her chin and, assuming a nonchalant air, wrote poetry.

One long poem described hospital life and included pictures of us sunbathing in our version of a bikini. It also mentioned the nurses and interns getting the beans for lunch, while we ate the strings. The morning Barbara and her friends finished the poem between giggles, we were getting ready for inspection, and the nervous young nurse was trying to keep us neat. Barbara read the poem to us and we all laughed; it was a funny poem. A fight developed over who got the poem next, and who would take care of it. They did not want it torn. The poem started around the room, each of us waiting patiently for our turn, but we were not able to move because our nurse was standing over us, just daring any one of us to mar the room's pristine cleanliness. Katie was trying to hand the poem to Irene when a gust of wind blew it into the hall. Grace hopped into the hall to pick it up and, as she leaned over, a plump white hand reached quickly forward and snatched it up. Grace, while trying to keep her balance, found herself nose to nose with the head nurse, who was coming in for inspection. We all gasped upon seeing Miss Hanna and right behind her, Miss Anderson, Director of the hospital. That poem had not been intended for official eyes. As Grace crept back to bed, those two stood reading. We remained in a state of shocked silence.

Those two women represented the height of authority in Mercy Hospital. Miss Hanna, her white uniform emphasizing her authority, was a heavyset woman who carried her head far back. The tiny nurse's hat with its narrow black band had to be firmly anchored to stay in place. Miss Anderson looked like one of the dignified pigeons on the porch. She always wore a dove gray, ankle-length silk dress with a severe white collar and cuffs. The dress had long sleeves, and she wore it both summer and winter. Her gray shoes had hightops and were buttoned on the side. She wore her dark hair in a neat bun at the back of her head and waved the hair around her face; this did not soften the sternness of her features. She wore glasses on a black ribbon pinned to her shoulder; she pinched these on her nose when she wanted to see the finer points of our bed making.

We waited what seemed like an endless time. Finally the women walked in, shoulder to shoulder, to Barbara's and Martha's beds, where they stopped. They smilingly told the girls they had written a lovely poem and told them they would have the poem printed in the *Nurses' Journal* if the girls would make a few changes in wording. We all sighed a breath of relief. The girls were to send the repaired poem to the office.

Sometime later our floor head nurse, Mrs. Smallwood, brought the *Nurses' Journal* to us, to be read by all. By the time the whole floor finished reading the magazine, it was in pieces. Mrs. Smallwood, on hearing that we had read the *Journal* to bits, brought a copy for each of the authors, which they wisely put away.

Daily Life at Mercy

The porch was fun, and since no one entertained us, we found ways to entertain ourselves. The boys could climb the posts and did so with encouragement from the nurses; they robbed eggs from the pigeon's nests. When the nurses left the porch we dropped the eggs through the wire mesh, trying to hit the little man peeling potatoes outside the kitchen door. Sometimes we hit him and he swore at us.

The doctors gave their time to the hospital and came once a week. These men were always in a hurry, but each child had the doctor's full attention for a few minutes, and each felt important for that time. We gave the doctors nicknames and used these among ourselves. A number of different doctors came to our floor. Dr. Schauffler treated our frame patients. He was very old at the time, and the nurses said he should give up surgery. He didn't.

Dr. Dennie was funny and joked with his patients. Dr. Francisco was a big, bluff man, but friendly, and Dr. Montgomery was a talkative man. Dr. Berger was my doctor; he did research on anemia. He was serious. He never walked; he always ran. He was large and wore a black mustache. His black, straight hair fell over one eye, and he had a habit of pushing it back with one hand. His face, by the time he had run up four flights of stairs, had a flushed appearance. He could be heard coming from the second floor puffing from the exertion. I heard the nurses say he would have a heart attack if he didn't slow down.

Dr. Berger was never unkind, but he treated me as a case, rather than a child. I always trembled when I heard his step on the stairs each Wednesday morning. His usual procedure after racing down the hall consisted of checking my chart at the desk, then seeing me. He rarely had any other patients on the fourth floor. After each visit, a new shot or some extremely nasty medicine appeared on my list. Also, new and unappetizing foods were suddenly on my plate at lunch, such as liver in congealed gravy. Yuk!

At this time I had no appetite and refused to eat even when the nurses made me stay an extra hour at the table, or when they fed me. Poor little John and Terry usually accompanied me. Four-year-old John was left-handed and ate quite well with his left hand, but the nurses insisted he eat with his right hand. At that time, until around 1960, left handedness was considered to be unaccerptable, and parents, teachers, and doctors always worked to force children like John to use their right hands. John ate slowly that way. Terry was a slow eater too, one pea at a time, and he chewed slowly.

Grace and George had name-calling contests at mealtime. They often became loud, and their bickering made an excellent cover for us when the nurse left the room. The child nearest the garbage pail was kept busy scraping our plates of food we did not like.

We loved breakfast. Hadi, the young black kitchen girl, made oven toast for us. We had to eat our cereal, and we did so while holding our noses, but then we could have unlimited toast with peanut butter and jelly. One day the boys ate fourteen pieces of toast each; that ruined our unlimited toast option forever.

August came, and the frame patients received new braces for their backs. This led to a lot of laughter because the girls were teenagers and wore only teddies for the fittings, and the young man who fitted them had curly black hair and a laughing, bantering way that the girls found irresistible. Martin worked carefully with his many queerly shaped tools, asking frequently if the pads fitted properly over the bad shoulder blade or bent back.

I would not have missed the fitting of braces. We all had fun, but those leather and aluminum cages with ties and padding did not look comfortable. I said so to Mae one day when she mentioned happily that she would be getting her finished brace in two days. She told me that without the brace she slumped far to the left side and the kids at school made fun of her. The brace made her look like other girls. She could then walk straight and get a job when she got out of school. Mae helped my understanding of the frame patients.

Each Sunday morning, the wards took on an expectant air of waiting for something pleasant to happen. The children who lived in the city could look forward eagerly to visiting day. The rest of us waited and hoped. My parents, in Warrensburg, wrote often, but came to see me only once during my three-month stay. Grace had not seen her parents for a year; they lived one hundred miles away in Nebraska on a farm and could not come to see her until she was released. She stayed in the hospital for three years until all her operations were finished.

We not only had visitors' day for our parents, but also a visitors' day when large groups of people whose money and works had helped the hospital were led through the hospital by a guide to see the children. These visits were on Thursdays. We disliked Thursdays.

Even less easy to ignore were the classes of young doctors brought in to study pediatrics. I can still remember the teacher lecturing the twenty or more students grouped around my bed (it seemed a hundred), surveying me with critical eyes. The teacher talked in technical terms that sounded like a foreign language to me. He sometimes turned my head from side to side or pulled down an eyelid to emphasize a statement. I sat there, under all those sharp eyes that seemed to bore right through me, and shivered.

When three long months had passed since I had come to stay in the hospital, Dr. Berger came to see me on his weekly visit and decided to send me home. I knew nothing about it until a nurse came in with my going-home clothes on her arm. We went down the main elevator, which was very slow. It was good to see Mom and to walk down the front steps to the street to catch a streetcar to downtown Kansas City.

Mom was short and heavy, with an endless supply of energy and happiness. We went shopping in Kresges for the first time and rode the old wooden escalator. I have liked escalators ever since then. We also rode a very fast elevator.

Mom took me to a restaurant, which was my first experience of eating out. We had prune whip for dessert, then we boarded a train for home. Such a wonderful day! No wonder my brothers and sister were envious of me. They and our friends considered me a woman of the world. My sophistication lacked something, but I did not dwell on that.

My various hospitalization times over the next five years added up to about six months of each year. That was a lot of hospital time for a child; it was necessary, but difficult.

Sick Again

Three months away from everyone had made me a stranger; the kittens had grown up and been given away. School had started and I had to change schools. I went back to the College Laboratory School where I had gone to kindergarten because the public school wanted to put me back to do second grade over.

I enjoyed the limelight that came from having been away and quite ill, but I was evidently very cross because a neighbor told Mom that if God took me it would be bad, but if I lived I would have to get along with the world. That was the end of any spoiling I had received.

At home I had a whole shelf to myself in the medicine cabinet. We learned that an olive cut the taste after a dose of mineral oil and made it possible to hold it down. More often than not my brothers ate all the olives, but hot salt water did the same thing, just not as pleasantly. Mom filled triple capsules with powdered iron so I could swallow them.

I could not stay well. January came and we were once again boarding the train in Warrensburg for Kansas City. Of course, Dr. Berger told us I must stay. Again Mom gathered up my clothes and I made the trip to Receiving Ward in the wheelchair for the very hot bath and a crib. Yuk!

A long week later, Dr. Berger came in to examine me, and I asked to go to the fourth floor. I learned to ask a question quickly, or he would be out the door and down the hall. Fortunately, there was an empty bed on the fourth floor, and I was moved there that day. A nurse brought clothing for me, and Grace was there so we picked up where we left off. We played hide and seek that night when the nurse left the floor for isolation ward. The linen closet made a good hiding place because the shelves were deep. I was a good climber and made it to the top shelves often. When "it" found me, I made a mad scramble to get down from the shelf and beat him to base. One evening I fell and bruised my arm. The morning nurse asked where I got the bruise, and I told her I didn't know. The truth would have stopped our evening games.

Grace and I spent two days behind the screen at the porch end of the hall catching up on the hospital gossip. This did not endear us to the bedridden frame patients. They made barbed remarks and passed notes, which we were not allowed to read.

Grace's doctor had promised her an operation to lengthen her short leg when she first came to the hospital. A year had passed and Grace was still hopping on her good leg with the cast from ankle to waist. She was very enthusiastic about the operation; she dreamed of not wearing an itchy cast and having two legs the same length. She could hardly wait. I asked whether the operation would hurt. She told me it would not and that an operation would be wonderful. She went right on bubbling about her long-awaited miracle.

Doctor Berger decided I needed a transfusion. He notified my parents that blood was needed and they should find a donor. They brought twenty-eight family and friends, but no one had my type blood. I was steadily getting worse. My parents were desperate; they asked to be typed. To everyone's relief, Mom had my type and gave the blood. The hospital did not like to take blood from parents of a large, young family, but after the first reluctance, the doctor began to call Mom whenever I needed a transfusion. Each time she gave blood, the nurses carefully guided her to the kitchen and stood over her as she drank a large glass of milk. We all laughed about that because Mom hated milk and never drank it.

I dressed every morning, but the nurses cautioned me to play quietly. I usually followed their advice and took books from our small fourth-floor library to read. Kind and grateful people had given those books to the library. There were books about many people and many subjects, from Tom Swift to religious tracts. I read them all. When I had finished, the nurses traded books with other floors. I had what seemed like an endless and varied supply of reading material.

I found a book on Christian martyrs. I read it while the other girls played the scratchy, wind-up Victrola. One story that proved most interesting was about a saint who suffered many tortures and was finally ground to pieces on a wheel. As I read it, Grace put on the "Habenera" from *Carmen*. To this day, when I hear that song it brings that book to mind. I had nightmares for some time after that.

The morning after I had finished that book, I had to have another transfusion. The prep nurses cleaned my arm from shoulder to wrist, then painted it with iodine. A girl named Barbara told me it was my war paint and the doctors would think I was an Indian and mistakenly cut off my arm. Everyone laughed. The nurses put me in a diaper and a sterile gown and wrapped a cloth around my head. The operating cart came with two nurses who told jokes all the way to the operating room, while I sat in frightened silence. It was nice to see Mom, but that lasted for just a few minutes. Dr. Berger came, put a needle in my arm as well as into Mom's, and left the room. The intern finished the transfusion and Mom left. Then I was taken back to fourth floor, but we sailed right past the ward door. I questioned that and was told that I had to spend the night in the cubicle in order to rest. They assured me that I could go back to the ward in the morning.

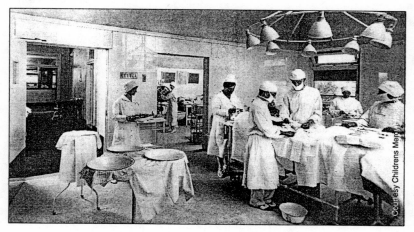

I had to stay in bed, but I felt so much better, I did not make a fuss. Transfusions must be all right, I decided.

Going to School

Going to school had many advantages. It kept our minds busy, and it left us with only an hour of nap time; in addition, I had heard of the joys of riding the freight elevator, and I was looking forward to trying it myself. I waited impatiently for the nurse to come by with our clothes on my first day back, and I picked the brightest dress I could find.

The routine temperature-taking had a bright moment that day because Grace hopped into the bathroom and dropped the thermometer into the bathtub by accident. She scooped up the mercury and stashed it in her stand. The nurse scolded her for carelessness. We did like to play with the mercury when the nurses were not looking.

The medicine nurse came in with her tray containing little glasses in orderly rows, each on a piece of paper with a child's name on it. It is surprising to me now to remember how docilely we took those medicines. There were no little pills, nor were the medications disguised with sweeteners or bright colors. The weekly cascara was bitter, though Barbara said it would move Rocky Mountains. Even I got a dose now and then in spite of my protests that what it did to my ever-present diarrhea was unmentionable.

Last came the cod-liver oil, and then we were ready to go to school. We all rushed to the elevator, but Grace held me back while the good elevator filled with boys in wheelchairs.

Nurse Strong opened the freight elevator door and the rest of us crowded in. She closed the door carefully, telling us to push the first-floor button. Down we went in total darkness, rattling, banging, and weaving. That was a wild ride. The boys added to the fun by saying they were sure the elevator was going to fall. After that first ride, I got out a bit shaken.

Our schoolroom had all grades, from first to high school. There was a special speech corner for the children with cleft palate. Some children were able to sit in desks and many were in wheelchairs. There were twenty-four of us that day. Our teacher, Miss Kearney, was white haired and neatly efficient in her lavender dress. She placed us new students in our grade levels. Those who had been there before immediately began to study in groups. My group of four girls learned the poem, "The Village Blacksmith." The time passed quickly. For recess we walked through the large playroom by the schoolroom, which had a pool in the center, to the yard behind the hospital. This place had a small amphitheater with tiers of seats for Fourth of July displays and other performances that came for us. We looked longingly at the swings and other equipment in the orphanage yard just over the fence, but our playtime was spent running races on foot, with crutches, and in wheelchairs.

We had a school holiday the morning Rin Tin Tin came to the hospital to do tricks for us. We all gathered in the Main Hall on the second floor for the show. Many came in beds; no one wanted to miss him because he was a talented police dog. We liked him and his trainer.

Highland Avenue school room

After seeing Rin Tin Tin, Troy, an older boy with a bad leg, made a pencil sketch of him and gave it to Miss Kearney. She had it framed and hung it in the schoolroom because it was a good sketch. Miss Kearney encouraged Troy in his artwork. He received his high school diploma that year. He was over 16 but could not go home until he finished a series of leg operations, so he stayed for three years. He drew with soft pencils for some time. Then Mrs. gave him oil paints and gave him the light room to work in for the summer.

The light room held a sun lamp, and during the winter we all took light treatments every day. The light room was a busy place after school and into the evening. One evening the nurse left me there too long, and I developed a bad burn on my leg.

Going to school made this hospital stay seem much shorter than the last one. At 11:15 we put our books away and walked or rolled out the door to be met by a nurse from each floor. We went out to the playground for recess or, in bad weather, went to a big playroom.

We had just enough time to wash our hands before lunch. Our appetites were better for the exercise. Then came our hour of rest before a nurse came by to take us back to school.

After three more hours of school, we came upstairs at 4:00 and were allowed free play. We really enjoyed this time and got pretty rowdy. Joe liked to lasso some of us and have us pull him around in the laundry cart. We were wild horses and tipped him over as often as possible. After tipping him over, we would run for our lives. One day I knocked over a clothes hamper, and the iron bar hit my nose. That hurt, but it got worse when Joe caught me easily because I was dizzy and he began to pummel me. The nurses were quite lenient because their shifts were almost over, so they turned a deaf ear to our uproar. Joe had a bone disease and died later.

I came up from school one afternoon to find Mrs. Smallwood waiting with good news. She told me I would not be going to school the next morning; I was to go home. I could hardly sleep that night and the girls caught my excitement, so we played cards by the hall light and discussed home until midnight.

It was a cold March day, but Mom and I were happy to be together and went straight home. The train gave me a headache, and I was glad when the trip was over.

It was good to be home and to have Mom reading to us in the evenings. My new young doctor had found a new way to test my hemoglobin, but I was not allowed to roller skate with friends at the college. Instead, I ripped wool clothing for Mom to make skirts and jumpers for school. Three more medicines were added to my already-long list, and they were evil tasting. Dr. Berger had suggested sun baths at home as soon as the weather permitted. Late in May, we took a rug and some ice water to the yard. The neighborhood kids joined my brother in the huge oak tree, and Mom read to us as I lay in the sun.

Life at Mercy Continues

In spite of all our efforts to keep me in good health, I went back to Mercy in September. It was hot; we'd had no rain for months. The dust storms from Kansas made the sun into a great bronze disk. Because we had no air conditioning, we slept on pallets in the yard.

At the hospital, I wasted no time getting to fourth floor. The heat in our ward had been so oppressive the girls asked to sleep on the porch. Miss Haloway, the head night nurse, said we could. We did not have much supervision and played until far into the night.

One evening the nurse came to push my bed into the ward, telling me I could sleep late the next morning. When I asked why, she told me a new test was scheduled and I would not be given any breakfast until after the test. I was frightened about this test. The nurse's explanation did not sound good to me, and being separated from the other children made me wonder what was going on. My active imagination went to work, but even that didn't prepare me for what happened when I woke up from the test. I opened my eyes to a green world; everything looked green. I picked up a book and tried to put my mind to the green print, but the color bothered me, and I could not concentrate on the story. The floor nurses were on the porch with sunbaths. I waited alone as time moved slowly along, but nothing happened. At 10:00, I decided to walk out in the hall to see what was going on. I heard the elevator stop, and I dashed back to bed. A nurse and an intern came in, put a screen around my bed, got out a lot of equipment, and cheerfully told me to swallow a little ball. That was hard to do. They soon walked out with the contents of my stomach in a jar; the equipment had been a stomach pump. My throat hurt badly. Miss Stevens came in to tell me they had set up a table in the hall with a special lunch, since I had missed breakfast. I slowly got out of bed and dressed and still more slowly walked through my still-green world to the table. They had gone to a lot of trouble for me and I appreciated it, but hard as I tried, I could not eat a bite of that nasty-looking green food. I do not remember telling anyone that the world looked green to me, and I doubt that it would have done me any good if I had. Adults at that time didn't take children seriously, and the nurse would have thought that a child who saw green was a bit peculiar! To this day, I don't know why I had a green day.

The next morning I woke up to a normal-colored day. We were still getting ready to go to the porch when we heard fire engines. Grace and I ran for the windows and saw the fire trucks turning in our street. We went to the porch and looked over the side; there was a fire in the laundry. We went back to tell the others where the fire was. More and more fire trucks came in until Independence Avenue had trucks lined up for two blocks. I had never before seen a hook and ladder truck. I was impressed.

That day was also my birthday. The mail nurse came in with a package for me. It was a wristwatch from Aunt Gladys. I put it on and walked around the ward showing off; no one else had one. One morning shortly thereafter, I woke up to find my watch gone. Grace and I hunted everywhere, but it was not to be found. Grace offered to hunt through the other stands in the ward; some of the girls let us hunt, but others did not. One thing led to another, and soon we were all accusing each other of taking the watch. When they took our morning temperatures at 9:00, we all had fevers. That meant they would take our temperatures every hour until the fevers came down.

Grace and I were still determined to find my watch. Some girls went through their stands with Grace and I watching, while others just argued that I was careless. We argued all day. I threatened to tell Mrs. Smallwood, hoping to scare the girl who took it into giving it back. Through it all, every hour on the hour a nurse came in to take our temperatures. At noon the nurse told us that either we were all coming down with something or our morning upset had caused our wholesale fever.

We remained sullenly silent. After a supper that everyone refused to eat, I started down the hall to Miss Swallow's office. I had not gotten far before Grace came hopping after me, telling me they had found my watch. I turned back and the watch was on my stand. I put it on and wore it day and night from then on. Our fevers subsided, and the nurses talked about the Mystery Fever for a week. We never did tell our secret.

The next day dawned sunny and hot, so we went back to the

porch. One end of the porch had a definite hill, where we could hold wheelchair races. We had those when the nurses were not around. The children who lived in chairs always won. We had a strictly enforced rule against anyone but the owner of a wheelchair being in it. This added element of danger made the racing even more fun. Some of us fell out of the chairs while racing.

We were always punished if we got caught breaking the rules. Our punishments varied, but they always included long, stern lectures. For those of us who could move around, we were sometimes put alone in the light room, or we missed Passing, or had to sit on our beds quietly, with nothing to do.

The rule against sitting in a wheelchair that was not your own was tested by one of the interns one morning. After checking charts and patients, he sat down in a wheelchair to read the paper. Miss Hanna and Miss Anderson came up on the elevator and silently walked down the hall behind him. We quietly observed the scene: Dr. Stockwell sat there in the sun reading his paper, not suspecting anyone was near as they walked up quietly behind him and stood there awhile. Finally he looked up, then went right back to reading. He looked up again, said "Good morning" to them, and continued to sit there while they reluctantly walked on. When they had gone, Dr. Stockwell sauntered into the building. After that, we all wanted him for our intern.

We children liked the porch; new things were always happening there. Just as we finished our sun bath one morning, a group of nurses came out, pushing a big bed, carrying a screen, and helping a young woman dressed in a bathrobe. The nurses were talking to the woman as she reluctantly got on her bed. One of the nurses brought me over to show her how brown she would be after a series of sun baths. We later learned she was a young nurse who had caught tuberculosis while working in the isolation ward. She was getting free treatment until she recovered.

When the noon trays came out, before we went in to eat, Grace and I were often kept busy throwing unwanted potatoes over the porch walls. We had to be cautious because the nurses were still carrying trays and feeding those who needed help. We had told the kitchen workers about our garbage pail escapades, and they saw it as their chance to get rid of unwanted food.

We were playing cards one night when we heard the nurse coming up the stairs. She was running, so we jumped hastily into beds. I had to jump high because by then I had a five-foot bed. I scraped my leg on the bed from my knee to my hip but did not dare squeak with pain.

Instead of checking each ward as we expected, she went straight to the kitchen. We could hear the banging of our tin drinking cups and pitcher. She walked silently on her rubber-soled shoes to the interns' door and laid the cups and pitcher down where the interns would fall over them.

We knew the interns were having a party in their rooms that night. We had seen two women come in at 8:00. The nurse ran back down stairs. Soon the emergency buzzer went off, and of course the first one out the door stumbled over the cups and pitcher. The buzzer went off a number of times that evening before the nurse came back to replace the cups and pitcher.

Sunday morning we all had a little trouble getting up. My parents came to see me, which was wonderful! They brought my brothers, whom I could see from the porch. They had to stay in the parking lot; they were not allowed into the hospital, but we were happy to see each other, even at a distance. I told my parents the story of the evening before, but they considered it to be a wild tale.

Back Home and Back Again

The series of tests started by the stomach pump brought a new diagnosis: hemorrhagic anemia. With the diagnosis came a whole new group of medicines. The medicine nurse threw up her hands in dismay when she read the list. There were not enough places on her tray for nine medications for one child! She solved the problem by lining all my medicine up on the kitchen counter. I tasted each and relined the little glasses from bitter to better tasting, with a glass of water at the end.

I also had to have another blood transfusion. They sent for Mom; she arrived, and I did get to see her for a few minutes.

The cubicle I vacated after that was taken by a sixteen-year-old boy. We tried to be friendly with him, but failed. The nurses said he was a cancer patient. We did not like him and made our dislike clear. Much to our dismay, he died after two months of suffering. We had not understood the situation.

We felt so guilty about our unfriendly actions to him that we burned our ribbons. These were highly prized and came on funeral bouquets that were given to Mercy Hospital after the bigger funerals.

Sunday Passing usually meant a special treat, so we looked forward to Sunday afternoon. One day the nurses hinted that that day was to be really memorable. Someone had donated ice cream to the whole hospital. It was a real treat. The only fly in the ointment was the Grapenuts added for crunchiness.

I had just finished my dish of ice cream when a nurse came to my bed with an arm full of clothes. I was going home. The girls said goodbye with a note of envy in their voices. I waved and called goodbye as I walked with the nurse to the elevator and then wished it would fly down instead of moving in its slow, easy manner. I could hardly wait to see Mom now that the time was at hand.

The hospital had taught me a number of things about the seamy side of life, and I learned many jokes from the girls and boys that a child my age should not have known. I became a menace to society each time I returned home.

After I had settled in at home, Mom felt I should be outside playing, but I had learned to enjoy reading and embroidering, plus resting. To get me some exercise, Mom instigated long walks for the whole family except Dad, who went fishing on the Osage River every weekend to get away from the pressure of business. Right after church that first Sunday morning I was back home, Mom let us call our friends and invite them for a walk and a picnic. We all pitched in to help make sandwiches. We ground up leftover roast, pickles, leftover baked beans, and anything else that was available, added homemade mayonnaise, and made a lot of sandwiches. The first hike took us to Hales Lake, a two-and-a-half–mile walk. After that, we walked many places on weekends, always with many friends. My sister Joan was only five years old when we started walking. The adults stayed with Mom and Joan while the rest of us went a little faster.

The Sunday hikes continued for years. In the summer we swam in the lake with Mom teaching us from the bank. Mom taught Joan and my brothers Andrew and Don how to swim from the shore, even though she didn't know how to swim herself. Finally, she bought herself a suit and taught herself to swim. We admired her determination very much; she was a talented woman who enjoyed life.

Sometimes in fall and winter we had huge bonfires on Bear Creek. Food cooked on a bonfire tasted good; even I ate well.

A good winter went by, and I felt reasonably well, although the stomach cramps from my constant diarrhea were hard to take. I also had headaches every day. One solicitous teacher sent me home every time she caught me holding my head, so I quit doing that. Staying home by myself was not my idea of fun.

Dr. McKinney kept a close watch on my blood count. When it went down to thirty, he suggested Mom take me back to Mercy.

It was back to Receiving Ward again. To make matters worse, there was no room for me on the fourth floor. I would not listen to anyone who suggested I go to the girls' ward on the third floor. The smell of ether from the operating room came up the stairway to fourth floor all too strongly. I could not imagine how overpowering it would be all morning on the girls' ward, which was on the same floor as surgery.

The nurses finally moved my crib, that hateful bed, to the very large ward on the second floor, near Receiving Ward. The children in this ward all looked ill. The girl next to me had just had an eye operation. She, along with many others, was cross and demanding of the nurses' attention. There were also more nurses on this ward. The child next to me kept crying, then reminding herself not to cry. She had orders not to rub her eyes, but she did it anyway. Nurses were constantly reminding her to keep her hands away from her eyes. Several of us jumped out of bed many times to stop her. After a week of bandages, her doctor came in to remove the bandages. We were all interested and were very glad to learn that she could see. We felt happy knowing we had helped the healing process. In fact, our celebration became so noisy, the head nurse, Miss Knight, came in to quiet us down. A generous Passing helped calm us, but we still felt like celebrating.

Two long weeks in that ward passed, then a fourth floor nurse came to push my bed to the elevator and up to the fourth floor, where I could dress, get out of bed, and enjoy life a little.

Grace

The nurse had taken me to the little girls' ward, but rules had relaxed and I was allowed to wear blue jeans and a shirt. Then I went to big girls' ward to find Grace. She had good news; she was finally going to get her long-awaited operation. She was more than ready for the surgery. When I went to see her, she had two huge peppermint sticks; she ate one while I ate the other. She was extremely happy, looking forward to two legs the same length with no heavy cast. I was not so sure her happiness was justified, but I did not say so.

Harry, a tall, lank boy, wanted to outdo Grace. He was scheduled for a tonsillectomy and bragged about how he would not ride the cart to the operating room and was so much braver than Grace. The next morning, the nurses prepped Harry and, dressed in his diaper gown and with a towel around his head, Harry waved to us as he started down the stairs. He fainted on the first landing. We understood; we were all fearful at times. Still, when he came back from surgery and woke up we all gave him a bad time.

While we were still in our state of preoperation euphoria, one of the nurses took Grace and me to the kitchen and gave us a treat. She sliced a lemon and gave us salt to eat with it. Fresh fruit did not appear often. We were quiet for the only time that week because the nurse told us to remain quiet since she had only the one lemon. The other girls questioned us about our time in the kitchen, but we did not tell, which did not add to our popularity that evening.

Bright and early on Saturday morning, the nurse came to prep Grace. This prepping was not easy because Grace was so excited, she could not sit still. Then she could hardly wait for the operating cart to arrive. She went down the hall talking happily to the cart nurses.

The morning dragged by. I walked the hall countless times from my ward to big girls' ward, unable to stay in one place. Lunchtime came and went, and then the operating cart came down the hall as I stood in the door. They took Grace to the cubicle. I looked in, but the nurse shooed me away.

Grace awoke in the night and I could hear her groaning. She continued to moan for the next three days. I spent my time wearing a path between her door and mine. I was not allowed in her cubicle. On the fourth day, the nurse coming out of Grace's door told me I could go in. I hesitated so long, she gave me a push and said I could not stay long. Grace and I both said hello and nothing else. Finally, I told her I would get her a book and went out terribly shaken to see how she had changed.

Neither Grace nor I ever mentioned her operation again. It had been too painful an experience. We were both disappointed to find that she had a new cast from waist to ankle. She had to stay in a wheelchair as she moved through the halls. Her doctor told her she had to wear the cast for six months, at which time she could graduate to two full leg braces. Grace became a somber child.

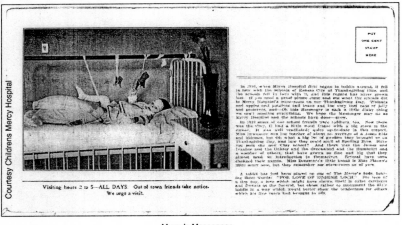

Mercy's Messenger

We had a new night nurse, who often told us she did not wear any underwear. We told her to prove it, and one night she did. That was a shock.

One ward on the floor was whispered about. It was said the children in it had a wicked disease that was inherited. We found out later it was the venereal disease ward, but the nurses of that time would not answer our questions. The babies and small children in this ward were isolated with a nurse on duty day and night. They were given hot baths several times a day. A few took sun baths but did not join the rest of us.

One of these children had beautiful long, black hair and had been in the ward for a long time. One day she went by us with a nurse pushing her bed. The word came to us from children who knew more than the rest of us that she had gone to First East to die. Within two days a nurse confirmed that she had died.

It was odd, but for some reason I cannot explain, we did not worry about death. It was all around us and we felt sorry for those who died, but it was a passing sorrow.

Grace had not smiled since her operation. She still stayed in her cubicle all the time, never got out of bed, and seemed sad all of the time. All of us noticed, so one night we asked the nurse if we could borrow the light cart. She said yes. We put two frame patients on the cart, Susan and Kitty. Sarah, a patient with club foot, and I pushed the cart down to the boys' ward where we made plans for entertainment later that evening after lights out. We told jokes and laughed a lot to cover the sound of our planning. The nurse let us visit Grace for a short while, and we told her to say awake. She told us she did not sleep well anyway. We just had to be patient and quiet until the nurse called, "Lights out in ten minutes." We hurriedly got the girls back to bed and climbed into bed ourselves.

Miss Farnsworth checked the wards in an hour, then went down the stairs. That's when we went into action. Sarah went to the bathroom to get a towel, and Lisa rummaged in her stand for a safety pin. Lisa had arthritis; her hands were fists, but she was included in our projects. I picked up colored glasses from Dorothy and a blanket from the closet in the hall. Sarah and I drew straws to see who would get to be a ghost, and I won. Sarah mounted guard at the stair's, and the boys were ready. I started down the hall. Just as I got to Grace's door, out popped the boys' ghost, in an Army blanket. He rushed at me, tripping on his blanket and knocking me down. The whole floor burst into laughter. It took some time to untangle ourselves, and there stood Miss Farnsworth with a severe look on her face.

With her silent disapproval over us, Bill and I went very quietly back to our rooms. Thank goodness for a nurse with a sense of humor. She went to the kitchen and made cocoa for all of us. We drank it and thanked her. While she did the dishes, we all fell asleep.

Sicker Than Ever

One morning I woke with my face hurting. I complained to the ward nurse. After one look, she rushed out the door. She came back immediately with Mrs. Smallwood right behind her. After looking at my tongue and asking me a few questions, she called for a thermometer. She carefully took my temperature and pulse. Mrs. Smallwood asked if they could call my Mother. I told her "Yes," then she wanted to know if there were other children in my home. I had two younger brothers and a sister. Her face fell. Then she asked how we would travel home, if I went. I told her we always went by streetcar and train. I asked if I would be going home. She said she did not know.

My answer arrived soon when a nurse came in to put me into a wheelchair and to push me to the elevator. We went down one floor to the Isolation Ward and went through a heavy door that swung shut with an air of finality. On either side of a long hall were glassed-in cubicles. The nurse pushed me past a ward where girls laughed loudly. I hoped to join them, but on we went, near the end of the long hall. She pushed me into a three-person ward with each bed divided from the other by a wood and glass wall.

The nurse put me into a crib and left. I looked around the room. Next to me, a very young baby gurgled. Then a young woman rose from her bed. It was a student nurse named Miss Brown who, like me, had mumps and had been sent to isolation. She wasn't supposed to be up, but she sat on the edge of her bed and talked to me. She dashed for her bed just before the floor nurse came in with thermometers.

The next three days passed quickly. The fourth morning of my stay in isolation, a large, red-faced nurse came breathlessly into our room telling Miss Brown that a man who said he was her husband had come, demanding to see her. Miss Brown burst into tears. Next came Miss Hanna and Miss Alexander, who stood over Miss Brown with their mouths pulled down in grim lines. They asked who the man was and asked whether she was married. Miss Brown told them yes. They then said she knew the rule: Student nurses had to be unmarried. Miss Brown had known that, but wanted to be a nurse badly enough to break the rule. Miss Alexander informed her that her clothes would be brought to her. Her nurse's training was over at that moment, and she had to go home to her husband. The two ladies made a hasty exit.

Miss Brown, still crying, got dressed while telling me she wanted to be a nurse so badly, she had lied to the nursing school. She didn't blame her husband for coming to find her. After she had been sent to the isolation ward, it had been impossible to call him, and he was worried.

For the rest of the week the baby and I made faces at each other. He got over the mumps and left isolation. Lucky baby.

I then had a private room. That meant long days with nothing to do and no one to talk to.

There were nurses coming in to take my temperature or to bring a tray. One pleasant surprise was that the dishes in isolation were blue willow, and I spent meal times admiring the plates.

Every time a nurse entered the ward, she had to put on a gown and wash her hands. On leaving, she washed her hands again and took off the gown. They explained the lack of toys and reading material by saying that anything that went into the isolation ward had to be burned. Time seemed to stand still. I had always been told I had a lively imagination, so I tried to tell myself stories for a week. Mom had always read to us at home, so I had something to base stories on.

The second week, imagination wore thin and I began to dread the long, sleepless nights. I started to hear peculiar noises in my closet; a door creaked, and my imagination did the rest. It got worse. I could not sleep day or night. I just lay there fearing to move, lest the thing in the closet jump out at me.

The night the door swung open, I had hysterics. As I screamed wildly for the nurse, I could see a white form moving toward my bed. A nurse finally came in and closed the closet door, explaining that someone had failed to close it. I remained unconvinced; I was positive there was something in that closet that was coming for me. The nurse became impatient and left the light on as she went to answer another call. That helped. After that experience I begged the nurses to leave the light on every night. Sometimes they did and other times they did not. Consequently, I did not sleep during those dark nights.

I stayed in the Isolation Ward for three weeks. As soon as I recovered from the mumps, I bombarded the nurses with requests for a return to the fourth floor. That was impossible, but I did not know that; no one had told me that the whole hospital had been quarantined. Finally, a nurse asked me if I wanted to go to a new ward that had just opened in First East for emergency operation patients. I jumped at the chance. Anything was better than staying in that dreary isolation ward by myself.

The same nurse came back with a new gown and took me to the new ward within the hour. The children were very ill, but so was I. I never appreciated others so much before.

The big bright ward held ten girls of various ages. I made the eleventh, so we were a little crowded. The nurse, as usual, put me in a crib. In four years of illness I had grown only in age; I was still small, so they still treated me like a baby in many ways.

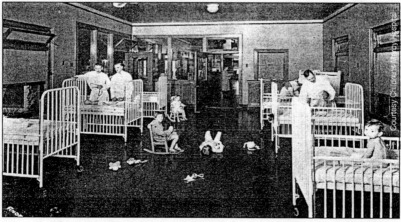

The ten girls were all happily counting the days until they would go home. Most of them would have to come to the out-patient clinic to have their dressings changed for a few weeks after their dismissal, but they assured me that was nothing. I had no idea when I would go home, but just having someone to talk to made me happy. I still had to remain in bed. We talked and sang for three days, then the girls began to go home, one girl a day. One Monday morning, I said goodbye to Tina and looked around the empty ward. The nurse had brought clothing for me and allowed me out of bed that morning. At noon she brought in a little table and chair and thoughtfully placed it near the hall door. I was slowly eating my lunch when Dr. Berger arrived. He was followed by an intern. They checked me. I hadn't seen Dr. Berger in awhile because he had not come to Isolation Ward. He jokingly told me I was a lucky girl to have a whole ward to myself. I put him straight on that matter in a hurry!

He seemed surprised by my outburst, but promised I could go home the next day, if mother could come after me. I woke up the next morning remembering Dr. Berger's promise.

I spent the morning with my nose pressed against the hall door, waiting hopefully for Mom. She appeared just before lunch. Shortly afterward, a nurse appeared with my street clothes over her arm. Even though I was in a hurry to dress and leave, I could not help handling the dress in surprise. I had never owned a dress so fine in all my life. It was made of the finest white batiste with hemstitching around the neck and short, slit sleeves. Across the top of the dress, Mom had done smocking in pink and blue. Above the hem was a flower garden of pink and blue French knots. I put on the white silk anklets and patent leather shoes, then told a nurse I was ready to go. Mom, never very demonstrative, took my hand firmly and smiled broadly as we started down the long front steps of the hospital, while answering all of my questions about home. I was ten years old.

I learned more about that dress later in life. Reports from Mercy Hospital about my health had gone from bad to worse. Mom made the dress and sent it to Maggie Burns, a seamstress, for hem stitching. Maggie did the embroidery as my reports continued to worsen. By the time Mom picked up the dress, it had become a work of art. They planned to bury me in it.

After I outgrew that dress, my sister inherited it, but she tore it at the neck. When she outgrew it, Mom put the dress away and we found it after her death. I have saved the dress; it is fragile, but it reminds me to be thankful for living.

Christmas at Mercy

Every winter I battled tonsillitis. At home I gargled, Mom swabbed my throat, and I still suffered. It was understood I had inherited this tendency from my grandmother. I even developed tonsillitis in the hospital the night of the ghost game, when I ran around the hall in bare feet. That time an abscess formed on my neck, and Dr. Berger decided to lance it. As I got on the operating cart, the nurses told me to be brave and be a good little girl. I waved to the other kids, and off we went to the operating room. As usual, I was scared to death. Operations at Mercy were, to some extent, informal. The doctors stood around me discussing which anesthetic to use. First they froze a part of my neck. Then they decided to put me to sleep. The next thing I knew, I was yelling. I stopped, and a masked nurse appeared, with soothing words. I thought the operation was still going on, but she told me I was ready to go back to the fourth floor. She took me back to the floor and the cubicle that had just been vacated by Grace.

That frightened me, for I wondered if the operation was worse than I had been told. I felt the bandage on my throat and it was small. I felt slightly relieved at that. There were two babies in the cubicle with me. I fussed when the nurse changed the bandage; she had to take out yards of packing and replace it. I received no sympathy from the nurse; in fact, she pointed out how nicely those little babies took the same treatment. They were perfect stoics.

Dr. Berger started coming to see me every day. I had to remain in the cubicle and in bed. I sat and read a picture book over and over again because no other books were available. The nurses promised to bring something else, but never remembered. I evidently was not allowed visits from the other children. Even Grace stayed away. I decided I must be dying.

One day Dr. Berger arrived at lunchtime. We had hot dogs that day and I had eaten very little of mine. He picked up the hot dog and asked whether these were served for lunch often. I answered truthfully, "Yes." His face turned a bright red, and he stamped out into the hall, shouting for Mrs. Smallwood. She came running. Dr.

Berger met her as she turned the corner from her office, waving the offending hot dog under her nose. "Why do you serve these indigestible things to sick children?" he bellowed. Everyone on the floor was listening. Poor Mrs. Smallwood could not get a word in. When he finally calmed down, she suggested he try the dietitian for an answer. She was shaken visibly. Dr. Berger went right to the desk, just outside my door, and called Miss Shirkey, the dietitian. Then he ran off down the stairs. We had no more hot dogs. That was a shame; we liked them.

I was bored stiff in that cubicle with those babies who fussed all day and night, except at bandage-changing time. I waited restlessly for night because then Sarah and Frances would come down pushing a wheelchair. They helped me into it because I was too weak to walk, and we went down to the big-girls' ward to play cards for the next three hours, diving under beds if the nurse came to check on us. The girls pushed me under the bed and hauled me out when the nurse left. I often got bruised on the iron frames in our hurry to hide. Wonder why the nurses didn't catch that?

I did not know it, but Dr. Berger had notified my parents to expect my death. He told them it was just a matter of time. Although no one told me I was dying, I suspected I must be quite ill from the length of my stay in the cubicle. I constantly asked to be moved to a ward. I did sleep during the day; my card playing at night was exhausting.

Gossip travels fast in a hospital. One night while playing cards I learned that a baby ward nurse from the third floor had been banished to the fourth floor. Miss Kelsey had been rocking babies for years. We could watch from Big Girls' ward. Some of the male baby doctors began to lecture her on rocking and spoiling the babies. Times change, they said, and she was going to have to change with them. But Miss Kelsey could not resist rocking a crying baby and continued to rock them. She was finally banished to the fourth floor. The thinking must have been, we decided, that she could not rock us.

Miss Kelsey was the kindest person I met in all my years at Mercy. She simply could not help pampering us. Each morning, Miss Kelsey braved the kitchen girl's wrath and prepared a poached egg on toast for me. She arranged it nicely on a tray and brought it in while it was still hot. How good it tasted! Thanks to her coaxing and extra care I did eat one good meal each day. Everything else tasted like old metal, and I could not eat it.

The girls often talked longingly about hamburgers served in a shop not far from the hospital. Food became our favorite subject of conversation. They did not expect to get any of those burgers because bringing in food was strictly forbidden. Occasionally, our parents smuggled in gum or cookies to us, and the lucky one always shared with the ward.

One night, to our amazement, Miss Kelsey came furtively up the stairs with a big box under her arm. I had dived into a bed, hitting my head on a metal bar, but when she opened the box the pain vanished, for there was a big, juicy hamburger for each one of us. Miss Kelsey knew of our nightly escapades. If anyone had told on her she would have lost her job. That would have been no small thing in those depression days. We loved her dearly and no one ever said a word.

We knew Miss Kelsey wanted to go back to her babies, for she talked longingly of them as she worked with us. We selfishly wanted her to stay with us forever.

The morning after our hamburger feast, I was rudely awakened by the prep nurse. I could not imagine why she was there. I asked questions and surprisingly received answers. She told me I was about to have my spleen taken out. She added that the spleen was just under my right rib. I remember Dr. Berger feeling under that rib, now that the nurse mentioned it. I sat there in shock after the prep nurse left. I did not like the idea of that operation one bit. Of course I had no breakfast, but as the morning proceeded, nothing happened. I kept asking every nurse who came in when I would go. They did not know.

Lunchtime came, and a nurse came in and told me they had just been notified that the operation had been cancelled. That was a close call, as I later learned, by asking questions. Children at that time lived an average of only five months after a spleen operation. The next day I went through the prep process again, but the nurse told me it was for a transfusion. I felt a lot better because it was to be a procedure I knew about and had been through before.

I had seen Mom for the few minutes before the transfusion so between that and the nurse's honesty about what was to happen, I

felt better. The day after the transfusion, Grace came wheeling around
the corner of the cubicle with good news. Clara was going home and
I could have her five-foot bed. I hated cribs. The nurse came with a
wheelchair to take me to the Big Girls' Ward. I rode down the hall on
cloud nine.

Once I got there, I had permission to get up and dress. It had
been a month since I had walked, so when I got out of bed that afternoon I fell flat on the floor. It took me a week to learn to walk again.
This did not stop Grace and me, for I could legitimately use a wheelchair to get around during that time, and we made the halls dangerous for pedestrians.

The minute I could walk, Mrs. Smallwood told me I could
go back to school. It was fun to ride the elevators with the rest of the
boys and girls and run noisily down the hall to the schoolroom, although many of us rode in wheelchairs or limped.

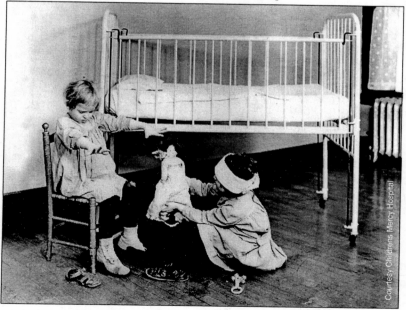

Christmas was only two weeks away, so we decorated the
schoolroom and sang Christmas songs. We also made decorations
for our wards from paper. We each sang songs in other languages; I
sang "Silent Night" in German, Eileen sang in French. Many of the

children spoke in German or Italian or other languages. Miss Kerney read stories of Christmas in other countries. We always enjoyed school, but especially around Christmastime.

All of the children who were well enough to be sent home left the week before Christmas, though most of them had to come back after the holidays. Those of us who were left felt alternately sad and excited. The year was 1931, and deep depression and drought gripped the whole country. The children told stories of getting nothing for Christmas in their homes. School proved a saving grace because it kept our minds and hands busy. The week went quickly.

Christmas found each of us putting a long black stocking on the foot of our bed with wire from funeral bouquets. We always drew straws for the ribbons on those bouquets, and those of us lucky enough to have a ribbon added them to the tops of our socks. It was whispered that the red ribbon Lisa owned came from a big-name gangster's funeral. Sarah said her family knew his parents well. While we worked on our stockings, we assured each other we were too old to expect anything in them.

We had planned to stay awake to see Santa, but the nurses fooled us and we fell asleep before he came. The next morning our socks hung limp and empty, but again we assured each other that we had not been expecting anything. The smaller children had full socks and were enjoying their contents loudly. We watched and laughed at their antics.

Nine o'clock came, and a nurse took all of us who could move, in any fashion, down to the first floor and into the large playroom. Santa came, giving gifts to all of us. Santa's gifts were dolls with little spool and cigar box beds, with mattresses and pillows to match. The boys received guns cut from wood, which pleased them. They ran through the crowded room banging at each other until the nurses took a firm hand.

While Santa made his rounds, I looked around at the children in the room. They came from all floors, and some had strange diseases. One child had a head as big as her body. She had long blonde hair with blue eyes, and she watched all the activity silently until Santa approached her. Then she clapped her hands as he stopped and talked to her.

A small boy sat in a wheelchair. He had a huge stomach;

however, he was shooting the other children with his gun and laughing. The boy with the cleft palate (one of Dr. Richardson's patients) also enjoyed his gun.

Grace and I could hardly wait to get upstairs and play with our dolls and spool beds. This was the only time I remember playing with a doll. When we got back to the floor, we found our presents from home on our stands. One wrapped present of mine was shaped like a cake. I opened it with bated breath, only to find a round, red doll overnight case. We all felt disappointed. We should have known it wouldn't be food since we all knew everything that was mailed to us was opened in the office, just to keep such smuggling from taking place. We got over our disappointment quickly, though, and we all talked happily and admired each other's gifts.

On Christmas Eve, Miss Shirley had come to each ward and asked us what we would like for lunch on Christmas Day. She had gotten an unanimous answer: Pie! She laughingly wrote it down in her book. The last time she had asked us about our food choice we had wanted carrot sticks in ice water. We discussed the chance of pie skeptically; pie had never been on the menu. But much to our delight, we had cherry pie for lunch dessert.

Christmas Day also brought visitors. Again I went out to the porch at the end of the hall to read behind the screen because my parents could not come. Those of us who did not have visitors had to find something to take our minds off of our loneliness.

I spent the afternoon reading over my letter collection and writing thank-you letters for my gifts. I also cried now and then. Christmas away from home had a lonely feeling. Grace did not have visitors either, but that day we were too sad to comfort each other.

Friends

The 1930's were hard depression days, and we felt it in many ways. Our parents could not travel the distance to visit us because there was no money for traveling. The children in Mercy told tales of hunger, filth, and such wretched ways of living, it seemed unbelievable to me. My family had clean clothes, even if they were well worn. We also had enough to eat, although it was often a pot of navy beans and ham hock. Many of the hospital children arrived terribly thin and hungry.

Children's Mercy Hospital 1930

Katey had been coming to the hospital for three summers to lie on a frame. Her father had committed suicide when he could not find a job, just the year before I knew her, when Katey was twelve. That summer, she had become thirteen and cried herself to sleep every night. She told of some rich people her mother worked for who wanted to adopt her. She liked them, but she prayed her mother would not be declared unfit by the court.

Beth told of the day she and her three sisters came home from school at lunchtime to find their mother sitting in the kitchen crying because there was no food in the house. Beth's mother had all of them kneel down and pray for food. As they prayed, a large bread truck came down the street, and miraculously a back door popped open, dropping a loaf of bread in the street. The children dashed out for the bread and were able to eat that day.

We all understood everyone had problems, other than our illnesses.

One night we were talking after lights-out had been called when a nurse came into the ward. We immediately became silent and hid under the sheets. She did not lecture us for talking, but came to my bed and dressed me in slippers and a bathrobe, which was most unusual. She said we were going to a student nurses' classroom downstairs. The bathrobe had very long sleeves, so she rolled them up and pulled the robe up over the belt to shorten it so I could walk to the elevator. We walked into a class taught by a doctor with twenty young nurses; I counted them. He motioned me to the teaching platform by his desk. With twenty pairs of eyes on me, I wanted to sink through the floor. The doctor began giving them my case history, which was a long one by then. I was eleven and had not grown in either height or weight for three years. He mentioned my sallow color, lack of appetite, and strength as typical of anemia. I had forgotten which type I had at the time; it changed each time I entered the hospital. He pulled down my lower eyelid to show the lack of color. As embarrassing as it was to be on display, his talk enlightened me on my disease. I was learning.

The student doctors had stood around my bed many times with the teacher talking at great length, with the young men asking questions. Both their questions and answers had been far beyond my childish comprehension, but student nurses were evidently nearer my level of understanding. The doctor told those nurses I had pernicious anemia. I looked it up in the dictionary. Bad news. The lecturing doctor used terms I could understand, and no student listened with more interest than I.

The morning after my visit to the nurses' class, I sat on my bed embroidering a pillow cover Mom had sent. Barbara had successfully taught me to do the backstitch. I had gotten my thread too long and was fighting knots in it, so when I heard Chris and Paula wind up the Victrola, I was ready to watch them do the Charleston. I had never seen that dance before. We enjoyed them and clapped when they finished the dance.

Chris and Paula were suffering from the aftereffects of pneumonia and spent hours every day blowing water from one bottle to another to strengthen their lungs. Paula blew her bottles faithfully and grew better. Chris began to get weaker. She could not get interested in the Charleston any more, although they always had an appreciative audience. She also lost interest in blowing her bottles. The nurses constantly reminded her to blow them. They compared her with Paula, but in a few weeks she just stayed in bed, too weak to walk. There she became even weaker, and the nurse finally came to push her bed to First East. When she died, we asked the nurses whether she would have lived had she stuck to the bottle blowing. The nurses shook their heads; they did not know.

One evening, Miss Trotter sent Grace and me to take our baths. We went right in and were joined by two others from the Little Girls' Ward next door. We were supposed to have only two in the bathroom at a time. The nurses shooed out the extra two girls, but they slipped back in. That night we soaped the floor and skated on it. Afterward, the nurses made us clean up the soap. It was hard work, so we did not try that particular activity again. We were lucky no one got hurt.

Grace thought we should soap the back of the tub and slide on it one night. We did, and we sloshed water all over the bathroom.

These bathroom escapades always led to disgrace and punishment. After the bathtub-soaping incident I cleaned the canary cage every morning for a month. Grace spent her mornings sitting on her bed in silence for a month. The girls in bed were ordinarily punished with long lectures and by having their lunch dessert withheld for a few days. These punishments discouraged us, but only for short periods of time.

Home For Good

When I returned home after my dramatic near-death experience, I received a lot of attention, not only by my family, but by people on the street who stopped me to congratulate me on being alive. I had permission to roller skate with my friend on the smooth college sidewalks. Central Missouri State University could afford better sidewalks than Warrensburg.

My parents needed a bill collector for their business, and since they lacked money to hire one, they decided on me. My bill-collecting career started at the age of twelve. I had not grown for three years, so I was very small, but out I went. I hated it. People did not have money to pay their bills, and I was lectured by professors, ministers, and businessmen, but I still had to go back and collect those bills. I did.

School resumed, but Dr. McKinney told us I needed to return to Mercy Hospital. I had to stay, as usual. After three days in the Receiving Ward I arrived on fourth floor in a wheelchair. Those trips from the Receiving Ward were the only times I could legitimately use a wheelchair. Everyone was sleeping on the porch at that time, so I joined them.

The boys were still laughing about the night they had a yelling contest to see if the nurse in isolation could hear them. The night nurse on the third floor did. She came right up and took them downstairs to her office. An emergency call came in before she could lecture them, so she left, telling them to stay there quietly until she got back. She did not come back for a long time, so the boys spread her fur coat on the floor and went to sleep. She lectured them soundly when she arrived in the wee small hours of the morning.

One morning Miss Kelsey came to the porch with three babies for sun baths. She still loved babies and rocked them every day. She felt especially sorry for one child with a cleft palate who would lose his first tooth when he had his surgery.

Mrs. Smallwood came to the porch one day and asked three of us if we would like to go to the zoo. None of us had been to the Kansas City Zoo, so we wanted to go. On the main floor of the hospital we met a man and woman who took us to their large, shiny car. We got to see the zoo and had some candy; it was a wonderful day. Back on the hospital porch, we had to tell every detail of the whole trip to the other children who had never been to the zoo.

Our night nurse listened to our pleas for food every midnight. She often brought us ice water; she was an unusually kind young woman. She made peanut butter sandwiches and did not fuss at us for staying awake or for our wheelchair racing. On the contrary, she usually sat down and ate a sandwich with us. For two lovely weeks we enjoyed ourselves at midnight. Then, one night while cutting bread, the nurse accidently cut a piece out of the brand new tablecloth. The next morning, during inspection, Miss Hanna and Miss Anderson spotted the cut tablecloth. They got poor, shaking Miss Able out of bed at the nurses' home and brought her over to the hospital. Faced with the evidence, Miss Able confessed to feeding the big girls peanut butter sandwiches on the porch at midnight, at our request. After finishing with our nurse, Miss Hanna and Miss Alexander came to the porch. They both asked us if we had asked for the sandwiches. We were frightened and told them everything. They told us we did not appreciate the help and care given to us by the hospital. We felt bad after they left; we knew the hospital with its doctors and nurses worked hard to make us well. Some of the girls cried.

Mrs. Smallwood, our head nurse on the floor, gave us a serious talk about following rules, mentioning the injury the frame patients could do to themselves by racing at night in the wheelchairs. We were a thoroughly chastened group of children. If the lectures had stopped there, we would have stayed repentant.

But they didn't leave it at that. The interns came out while we were taking sun baths and told us how necessary sleep was for ill children. About halfway into their lecture, Grace smiled. The intern who was speaking at the time told her to get that supercilious smile off her face. She hid her face in her pillow until he stopped talking.

The interns left, walking purposefully, like men who had done their duty no matter how distasteful it had been. The girls sent me into the building to hunt up the new word "supercilious" in the dictionary because we did not know what it meant. I was still wearing my sunbathing breechcloth, so I pulled my dress on over my

Author Bea Johns on the right

head and ran in to find the word. I returned to find the head night nurse, who must have been asleep when the interns were there, giving her blistering, though short, lecture. She walked away with Mrs. Smallwood, saying with a laugh as they got to the door, "You know I don't blame them; I like a sandwich at midnight myself." Three day-nurses gave us another lecture in the afternoon. We began to think we had accomplished something enormously funny. When Dr. Francisco came out to add weight to the lectures, we burst into laughter. He left in a huff.

Shortly after the porch upset, I went home. The year 1932 was my last visit to Mercy. I went into remission for most of my teens. Even if I had needed to go back, I could not have done so. The early doctor's wife had reported Dad as having too much money in fishing tackle, but that was based on some sort of misunderstanding. Small towns can be hot beds of trouble and gossip. Dad's fishing tackle was all second hand and very cheap. Ah well, the hospital had been there for me when I needed it, and I had stayed alive.

The year 1928 saw my health hit rock bottom. I became a patient in Mercy Hospital that summer at age 8. Warrensburg, Missouri had a college that educated young people, but doctors and hospital space were sparse. Few of us had money, and illness often caused death. My parents did not accept that as an option for one of their children, so they did something about it.

Mercy Hospital saved my life a number of times over a period of five years. It was an unusual experience in many ways, so it was worth writing about.

I never heard from Grace again. When I left the hospital the last time, she had not yet mastered walking with her heavy braces. She was using two crutches, and the doctors said she could go home as soon as she could walk without crutches. She was working hard at it, but after her miserable operation, she was having a hard time of it. I have thought of her often and wished I had gotten her address.

When I turned sixty-six, after many diagnoses and fifty-one years of suffering, my disease was found to be Crohn's disease. It is a disorder that makes the person double up with cramps after meals. The patient also has diarrhea, bleeding of the intestines, and fevers. Many people have died with Crohn's disease. There are many treatments for the disease now, although the research has been done mostly on men, by men. The disease acts differently on women, yet we are treated with the men's research. Unfortunately, when I protested this to the Crohn's CEO in New York, I was called names.

My disease had always been the same; it was just given many names when I was a child, before much was known about Crohn's. I have had no intestinal operations. Whenever they were offered, I left the doctor's office and did not go back. A lot of people died of these endless operations in those early days.

Like all of my friends, I worked my way through college; all of us became teachers. Central Missouri State University was a teachers' college. I have a Bachelor's degree in education, a Master's degree in language arts from Webster University in Webster Groves, and thirty-plus hours in graduate physical education from the University of Missouri-St. Louis. In 1941, I married John P. Johns and had three children, two boys and a girl. John died in 1969 and I went on teaching and raising Candy, my youngest. It has been a busy life. Our three children are now grown and productive adults.

Candy, Eric, Bea, John, and Gerald Johns in the early 1960s

I am now 76 years old; I travel, play golf, cycle, swim, and take part in the Senior Olympics. Pain has always been a part of my life. I am not a hypochondriac, but I do have to live carefully. I travel, but I must always watch what I eat. In 2002, I nearly died twice of kidney trouble. If I am like a cat, I have used up all of my nine lives and am starting on the second nine. But thanks to Mercy Hospital in those critical years of my life, I am living and enjoying life.

Try A Greener Day